OVERLEAF LEFT A view of Venice showing the
embarkation of Niccolò and Maffeo for their
first journey. From an English manuscript
(c. 1400), *Les Livres du Graunt Caam*
(MS Bodley 264, f 218).
OVERLEAF RIGHT A Chinese pottery figure
of an actor. Yüan dynasty, AD 1271-1368.

Marco Polo

Richard Humble

Introduction by Elizabeth Longford

G. P. Putnam's Sons · New York

For Wenny

First American Edition 1975

© George Weidenfeld and Nicolson Limited
and Book Club Associates 1974

Art editor Andrew Shoolbred
Layout by Florrianne Henfield

Filmset and printed Offset Litho in Great Britain by
Cox & Wyman Ltd, London, Fakenham and Reading

SBN: 399–11473–4

Library of Congress Catalog Card Number: 74–19870

Contents

Introduction 7
Author's Note 9
1 The Unknown 13
2 Mission 35
3 Crisis 49
4 To Hormuz 68
5 Across the Gobi 88
6 The Great Khan 115
7 Lord of Cathay 142
8 Back to the West 173
9 Home 191
10 Achievement 213
Further Reading 224
List of Illustrations 225
Index 229

Introduction

SIX CENTURIES AGO the *Travels* of Marco Polo were synonymous with tall stories, the taller the better. It was not for nothing that he earned the nickname of 'Marco Millions'. Marco had seen millions of marvels which his contemporaries found hard to swallow. Yet this young son of a Venetian merchant (he was sixteen when his father and uncle first took him on his travels to legendary Cathay) was in truth a record-breaker. He lived during a unique epoch – the zenith and decline of the Mongol Empire – and served a human phenomenon – Kubilai Khan. Many places which Marco saw were not seen again by Europeans until last century.

We are introduced most effectively by Richard Humble to the horrifying tempor of a civilized world suddenly threatened with extinction by Mongol hordes from China. One papal bull struck a characteristically doomwatch note when it foresaw 'wars of universal destruction'. Besides the Mongols, or Tartars, there were other centres of violence, such as the Mamluks, the robber-armies of the Karaunas, and the terrible Moslem 'Assassins', whose name was derived from *hashashin* – hashish-eaters. Having placed the three Polos in this perilous setting, Richard Humble rightly leaves Marco to tell the story of their journeys in his own words. And beguiling words they are. Marco possessed enthusiasm and a photographic memory. Among so many colourful curiosities, I particularly like the fathers of Vochan who looked after their new-born babies for the first forty days, because their mothers, in carrying them for nine months, had already done more than their slaves. The greatest interest of all, however, attaches to the Court of Kubilai the Great Khan.

Richard Humble describes Kubilai's empire as 'a model of enlightened and beneficial rule'. In this he agrees with Marco, who was happy to advise Kubilai as a 'travelling privy councillor' for many years. Christianity was one of the religions which attracted Kubilai. But whereas modern Christians are apt to baulk at miracles, Marco's problem was to provide a miracle for the Great Khan.

Kubilai's summer palace according to Marco was built of split bamboo held firm by silken guy-ropes. This airy dwelling, together with its owner's handsome face, 'ruddy as a rose', compares favourably with the 'stately pleasure-dome' in Coleridge's *Kubla Khan*, and so do the descriptions of the unbelievable splendours of Kubilai's Court. Nevertheless Kubilai had his own colossal weakness. He could not resist further conquest. Richard Humble thinks Marco may actually have seen Kubilai's final, disastrous attempt to invade Japan, when the islanders were saved by a cyclone, *Kamikaze*, the 'Divine Wind'. All in all, we have something like two Great Lives in the story of Marco Polo: Kubilai Khan as well as Marco himself.

Though no scholar – Marco missed out completely on the *printed* books at Hangchow – he has left us a classic not unworthy of his famous predecessor, Herodotus. Both had the journalist's flair and the same guileless air which seems to say, 'Swallow that if you can. Deny it if you dare.' There are far fewer people today who would deny the truth of Marco Polo's tales than when his best-seller first swept Europe. Many of his tallest stories have been substantiated: the strange oil in Baku which was not 'good to eat' but many came to fetch, and the fireproof cloth spun from rocky fibre, though no one has yet seen the monstrous birds which dropped elephants from a height and devoured their broken carcasses. Marco's *Recollections* are for every reader, from the oldest to the youngest. We should all like to have gone with Marco Polo. Richard Humble's book makes us feel that we did.

Elizabeth Longford

Author's Note

MARCO POLO dedicated his incredible account of what he saw and heard of on his travels to 'all people who wish to know the various races of men and peculiarities of the various regions of the world', and so the correct title was and should be *The Description of the World*. But it is basically a book of travels without which it is impossible to tell Marco's story: constant reference to it is essential. I therefore refer to it as 'the *Travels*' throughout this book for the sake of clarity.

R.H.

ند ندموا على مخاذلة ايلكخان وانهم يعتذرون عن ذلك وىرىدون

ولم يبق له نوم ولا قرار فخرج من بينهم ومعه سبعمايه فارس

مرا بان ىوضع التبن على الجليد ىوضع ثم عبر فلما وصل اليهم عنكر

1 The Unknown

IN THE OPENING DECADES of the thirteenth century AD, the
civilized world reeled under the onset of a new and terrifying
threat to its existence. No such phenomenon had been known
before then; nothing like it has ever been seen since. Across the
entire land-mass of Eurasia came the Tartars of Mongolia in their
thousands, commanded by ruthless and gifted leaders driven by
one simple motive: to conquer the world. They fell upon the
ancient empire of China and conquered it; they overran the whole
of southern Russia; they reduced Persia, for over a thousand years
the traditional enemy of the West, to servitude; they pushed into
eastern Europe and smashed its hosts in pitched battle. Like the
Goths and like the Vikings who had come after, the Tartars were
regarded as a scourge of God, a calamity of unprecedented dimen-
sions. In the year 1260 Pope Alexander IV, true to his role as
the spiritual leader of Christendom, issued a warning to every
Christian ruler – a message known from its opening words as the
papal Bull *Clamat in auribus*:

> There rings in the ears of all, and rouses to a vigilant alertness those
> who are not befuddled by mental torpor, a terrible trumpet of dire fore-
> warning which, corroborated by the evidence of events, proclaims with
> so unmistakeable a sound the wars of universal destruction wherewith
> the scourge of Heaven's wrath in the hands of the inhuman Tartars,
> erupting as it were from the secret confines of Hell, oppresses and crushes
> the earth. . . .

Despite this sonorous message of woe, it soon became apparent
that Christendom was not, in fact, doomed. The Mongol hordes
were led by a supreme overlord – the Great Khan – and when this
worthy died, the Tartar leaders had to trek back over two thousand
miles to their barbaric capital at Karakorum, in the heart of
Mongolia, to elect a successor. Jenghiz, the first Great Khan, died
in 1227. Of his four sons – Juji, Chagatai, Ogadai and Tului – Ogadai
was eventually proclaimed Great Khan. He reigned from 1227 to
1241 and was succeeded by his son Kuyuk, but no direct hereditary
line emerged. Kuyuk died in 1248 and the next Great Khan elected
was his cousin Mangu, the son of Tului. By the time of the reign of
Mangu Khan (1248-57), the vast extent of land which the Tartars
had conquered had already been parcelled out into subordinate
khanates and the process was continuing into its inevitable sequel:
the emergence of semi-independent powers.

One of the earliest prominent western khans was Mangu's contemporary Batu, who defeated the Polish-German host at Liegnitz,

PREVIOUS PAGES A page
from a Persian manuscript
showing Mongol troops
crossing a frozen river.

OPPOSITE Jenghiz Khan on
his throne. From the
fourteenth-century Persian
manuscript of the *Jami
al-tavarikh* of Rashid Ad-Din
Sinan, 'the Old Man of
the Mountains'.

13

The Tartar Empire

Superb horsemanship, not numbers alone, was the key to the sweeping victories of the 'Mongol hordes'. Their high tide of conquest reached as far west as Germany and Poland before it became apparent that the Christian West was not, in fact, doomed to destruction.

Unchallenged masters on horseback:
RIGHT Jenghiz Khan's cavalry, from a contemporary painting.
OPPOSITE A Mongol warrior plaits the tail of his horse – a charming expression of the Tartar bond between man and beast.

BELOW The death of Jenghiz Khan, the founder of Tartar domination, from a Persian manuscript.

Silesia, in 1241. Fortunately for central Europe, the year of the disaster at Liegnitz was also the year of the death of Ogadai, the Great Khan, and the Tartar host pulled back to the east. During his retreat, Batu reduced Bulgaria and the lower Danube provinces of Moldavia and Wallachia. He finally established himself on the lower Volga, carving out the khanate of the 'Golden Horde'. The 'Golden Horde' territory reached westward beyond the Dnieper river into Poland, north to the Russian republic of Novgorod and south to the Crimea and the Caucasus mountains. Across the Caucasus lay the ilkhanate of Persia, founded by Mangu Khan's brother Hulagu. He was one of the most famous Tartar commanders, smashing the Persian caliphate with the capture of Baghdad in 1258 and pushing south-west into Syria. When Hulagu tackled Mamluk Egypt, however, he soon found that he had his hands full. Succeeding where the Poles and the Germans had failed at Liegnitz, the Mamluks inflicted a resounding defeat on the Tartars in the battle of Ain Jalut in 1260. Egypt, the last Moslem province left in the Middle East, was saved from Tartar rule. Hulagu pulled back into Syria and Mesopotamia. His territory was still vast, stretching east along the Persian Gulf coast to the Indus river and north to the Aral Sea.

At the other end of the Mongol Empire, the Tartars kept up the pressure on the faltering resources of the Chinese Sung Dynasty. Jenghiz Khan had conquered the kingdom of Hsi Hsia, the westernmost bastion of the Chinese Empire, and forced back the Chinese to the Yellow River. Korea fell in 1231, and Szechwan province seven years later. But it was in the reign of Mangu Khan that the first official Tartar viceroy for subjugated China appeared on the scene. He was Kubilai, Mangu's brother, and he made his mark by smashing the southerly province of Nan-Chao in 1252-3. In 1257 the Mongol capital in China was established at Shang-tu, to the north of the present site of Peking. In the following year, while the hosts of Hulagu were taking Baghdad at the other end of the empire, Kubilai's forces were pillaging as far south as Hanoi. As effective ruler of the largest province of the Mongol Empire, Kubilai had no trouble in securing his election as khan by his own army after the death of Mangu. What time would prove to be one of the most remarkable reigns in history had begun. Carved out by force though it was, Kubilai's empire may still be described as a model of enlightened and beneficent rule.

Such, in brief, is the story of how the great Tartar principalities fared after the death of Jenghiz Khan in 1227. Little or none of

OPPOSITE Jenghiz Khan seated in a mosque at Bukhara. Before him stand two Moslems. From the *Jami al-tavarikh*.

۹۰

مکتاب و ضع و طلع ازاین روی و معارف هندی که حضرت آمد جبنه طالعه شرایی و صیاد برشت و بشرف آن و ماطبع بانی و درش مطوف با استاد و لبس بازنده قسای رهمذرباین مویده که ازمقام رهای بانان است کند خانه خدا است از اسب مرن آند و مردوسه با بهمیر آمن و مرمون که هجول از علان قسمت انسان را مانکم و مکتبدرا بتا بهای شهزبکنا ذلد وعلاي مي کشنه و صنادن صابق اطراي و خیاها و شراب درمجی بند باخته و منیان شهر باحاضر کردابهان با سلاع و درص مي کردند و معوقن با سول علایش او زمرکینه و اعیان زو سادات رابه وعلما بابه تجاری سنور بانان بوسرطولیله مجا فلت استاد اسبان استاده و استان احکام آن افوام رابه احمام کرد و لعنه از زازا عموم اصل شهریا حا فذرابند و مرمند مصلی عبدرت و لعذار تری خلاف و لذر سلطان لن فرمح مام کننای من بانبان که بناحنا کاها بزرگ کرده ابند و بزدکان نشار کرکا و منم اثنا اثن جریده ید از این جمعن بعد دلیل مي کرم سبب المک مندا حندا ام آن کا کاها بزرگ نباین درکی مرد کجدای حون من عدای هرینما لرشا ذی دعوان رابس ابنده اذ اسا و معتدان نکا کیسند هرکه معقا حضر دراره لکشنه و اسم با سنای چهف ریک معروی و رکی معن کرد المکارنه کاسکران استارا لزصی رابدان را کاں کشند و واعیان زبان کرد کرسط عان و نراالغان را طلب دانت و رفرید ناما لها و ممون رابه مم

دوت و رفضاد کری باهش کرد این صددنود شربی و باتح غنیب و بوغن غزا رهان مطالبی ما از معتدان استان ذنسا بر خی و بازار مي شنه و زباد تمکلیفی و موانندی مي جمو بی نه و فرود تا اش بود محلات درنه و منه بهر محل دور سوخته نه بعر فر اصابع و بنشی باها که زاآهرمود و درمم و مریم تکار بعد جهارا برانبه و انطا بین معنینها را استورند و کا بخاره آورد و کا بمیر بر بنذ و وار اندرون نا درون نا لعظم با مراهنه و دره رها مراں جمله مکا رحمت مکرند ماعاقبت اصل جهار رابکار بانطار رسند و جند و صص بمهادات جیوبات بازنین شنوی شد در مر از جر خی بکارا ۰۰۰۰۰ مصل را بار کشنه در فلعه با انن در زد د بانه با بالای نگماشتن زیا و فن از یک دهر بقبل آمده و زمان و کلوتکان نا ابنده با بنده حون مرده مرده تنراز اطفا مها برخال لرابند ابها

موریلتای بزرک چنگیزخان نومی سیده نه باید بصه فیروز و لقب چنگیزخان برو مقرر

وعزیمت اوچنگ بیروق باژناه کیکسه لهان وکونتن بزرق خان هذ کردرا چون مبارکی و فرخی مارس سال که سال یوز مایند بوافق

یب سنه اثنین وسمایه هجری در آمدیم درا اول مصلحار چنگیزخان فیروز و ناومنی نه باید سید بابای کردند محمیی باعطت

مورلیتای نزدک ساخت ودران موریلتای لقب بزرک چنگیزخان ن بدوی معز کردند و مبارکی بخت نشت

these events were known to Christian Europe. The Tartar irruption into eastern Europe and the defeat at Liegnitz in 1241 was a traumatic shock which was not forgotten overnight, and it was not surprising that Pope Alexander IV's unnecessary trumpet-call of doom coincided with the accession to power of Kubilai Khan at the other side of the world.

Yet the energy and ebullience of thirteenth-century Europeans was never more clearly shown than by the speed in which shrewd and far-sighted European *entrepreneurs* – political, religious and mercantile – adjusted their attitude towards the awe-inspiring new power which had towered up in the East. Within a few decades the Tartars had shattered the old, familiar world and built a new one. Hitherto the traditional foe in the East had been the Saracens in the Holy Land; now their power lay in the dust. In its stead, stretching to the furthermost bounds of the known world and beyond, stood this huge new empire. It was ripe for political negotiation. It was virgin territory for Christian evangelists. Above all, the merchants knew that fortunes lay waiting for those who would prove hardy enough to take the plunge and make contact with the Tartar overlords. And when it came to economic incentives, the state most immediately interested was the Republic of Venice and the hard-headed financiers who directed its fortunes.

Since the late eleventh century the major ideological obsession of Christian Europe had been the Crusades: the liberation of the Holy Places of the Middle East from the infidel rule of the Saracens. This cause had attracted the cream of Europe's fighting men for more practical reasons: land-grabbing and castle-hunting. The persecuted Christians of the East and the impassioned exhortations of the Church proved insufficiently strong arguments to overcome human nature. Subsidized military expeditions under the leadership of top commanders – with the bonus of promised spiritual salvation thrown in – offered an irresistible chance to break out of the restrictive crust of established Western society. To put it bluntly, the Crusades were the ideal opportunity for soldiers and administrators to become big seigneurial fish in a smaller, new feudal pond of their own making. From a practical point of view the Crusades became a joke. The Third Crusade, for example, broke down because of the insuperable natural rivalry between King Richard I of England and King Philip Augustus of France. But the Fourth Crusade – which lasted from 1202 to 1205 – was nothing more than a blatant act of international crime, and in this crime the Republic of Venice was the prime mover.

OPPOSITE Jenghiz Khan pictured with two of his sons, Ogadai and Juji. Ogadai succeeded to the khanate. From the *Jami al-tavarikh*.

19

OPPOSITE While the Mongols terrorized the eastern and Asiatic races, the Christians of Western Europe were crusading against Islam in the Middle East. The religious intent of the Crusades was a mask for the private ambitions of many European princes and lords. This page from the thirteenth-century chronicle of Alfonso X of Castile shows Arabs and Christians in battle.

LEFT A contemporary illustration of a Crusader knight doing homage.

OVERLEAF An aerial view of the magnificent Crusader fortification at Krak des Chevaliers.

The Mediterranean Sea offered the cheapest, the quickest and all in all the most efficient route by which to convey a fighting army to the Middle East; and for this ships, provisions and money were naturally essential. The Republic of Venice, having established itself as the leading Christian power in the Mediterranean by a process of evolution not relevant here, was the natural candidate

Crusaders departing for the
Holy Land: an illumination
from a medieval manuscript.

for the job. Its leader, the Doge Enrico Dandolo, undertook to
supply the necessary ships and supplies to the Crusaders in return
for hard cash and a half share in all conquests made during the
venture. When the money was not put up on schedule, the
Republic engineered the perversion of the Crusade into a full-
blooded plundering of the Byzantine Empire, with Venice once
again taking the lion's share of the profits. The victim could well
have been Moslem Egypt – despite the fact that the Venetians had
been trading with Egypt for years and would have had to weigh
up the effects of their possible loss of this lucrative trade monopoly
– but Constantinople was nearer. It was also a much richer target
to plunder. Machiavelli himself could not have done better. An

A medieval illumination showing a knight receiving his sword from the king.

understanding of the brass-tacks *Realpolitik* practised by the Venetian leaders helps explain why the first positive moves to make contact with the Tartars on a commercial basis came from Venice. And the first Venetian merchants to penetrate the heart of 'Tartar country' were the brothers Niccolò and Maffeo Polo, in the 1260s. On this journey, as will be seen shortly, they met Kubilai Khan in his capital; and their first journey led to their second, on which they were accompanied by Niccolò's son Marco and his photographic memory.

Although the Polo brothers blazed a trail of their own on their first journey to the East, they were not the first Europeans to visit the Tartars on their home ground – a fact which is still generally

25

overlooked today. At least two extremely brave (not to mention energetic) Franciscan friars had already made the wearisome and dangerous journey to Karakorum and returned safely. The first was Giovanni di Piano Carpini, sent out by Pope Innocent IV in 1245, and the second was Guillaume de Roubrouck, an emissary of Louis IX ('Saint Louis') of France, who followed Piano Carpini in 1253.

Two broad land routes, running north and south of the Caspian and Aral Seas, led to the heart of the Mongol Empire around Karakorum. Both friars took the northern route, first crossing the territory of the Golden Horde and then heading into that of the neighbouring 'White Horde' (a smaller province founded by Orda Khan, another grandson of Jenghiz). Skirting the northern shore of the Aral Sea, they next entered the central province of the Mongol Empire, the khanate of Chagatai, which embraced Turkestan and extended to the western fringe of the Gobi Desert (then called the Lop Nor or Desert of Lop). The friars headed north along the northern edge of the Gobi to Karakorum itself, and virtually retraced their route on the return journey. Roubrouck's route differed from that of Piano Carpini in two respects. Carpini had set off overland from Germany, down the Danube into Hungary and then north-eastwards into the Ukraine; Roubrouck, setting out from Acre in the dwindling Latin kingdom of Jerusalem, headed for the port of Sudak in the Crimea via Constantinople, journeying by sea. And on his return journey Roubrouck headed for the Aral Sea north of Lake Balkash instead of south. He was thus treading the warpath taken by the great Tartar expedition of 1236, which swept westward from Mongolia to the Volga.

The journeys of the friars were made before the great stabilization of the central and eastern Tartar territories under Kubilai. But they did prove that even a comparatively uncultured Tartar warlord like Mangu Khan was quite willing to receive emissaries from the Western world. As missionaries bearing the message of truth from Christ's Vicar on Earth, Piano Carpini and Roubrouck achieved little or nothing. They also found to their surprise that they were not even true pioneers, for Europeans had preceded them to Karakorum – men about whom the historical evidence is maddeningly vague, but who seem to have found employment at the Tartar capital on account of their military and technical skills. But the friars can nevertheless claim the honour of being the first official missionaries from Europe to Mongolia on record.

The Polos' motive for their first venture to the East was totally different: money. As early as the period when the friars had started out, a fairly secure route had been opened up from the Black Sea to the lower Volga, and the Tartars of the Golden Horde were well used to European visitors. The port of Sudak, on the south-eastern coast of the Crimea, had become an established 'advance base' for Western travellers and traders. At Sudak there was a colony of Venetians; at Sudak, too, Niccolò and Maffeo Polo's brother Marco had a house. Thus Niccolò and Maffeo were extremely well placed for the first leg of the trading enterprise which they undertook in person 'in the year of Our Lord 1260, when Baldwin was Emperor of Constantinople and Messer Ponte governed the city in the name of the Doge of Venice'. A good year, in short, for *entrepreneurs* from Venice heading east, with the Black Sea virtually a Venetian lake.

This first journey of the Polo brothers has been mapped out for us by Marco the younger in the Prologue to his own famous book of travels. Niccolò and Maffeo Polo's first port of call was Constantinople, where they got together the stock-in-trade for their venture. Marco describes this as 'many jewels of great beauty and price'. It was clearly a sophisticated version of 'beads for the natives'; certainly a costly investment, but one easy to make in one of the capitals of the civilized world, and one on which the brothers obviously intended to reap a fat profit. With this costly cargo they sailed to Sudak, got together a caravan of transport beasts and headed overland into the broad steppes of the Golden Horde.

Clearly, too, the Polos had little trouble in reaching the capital of the ruler of the Golden Horde, Barka Khan; as Marco rather loftily puts it, they 'rode without encountering any adventure worthy of note until they came to the Court of Barka Khan'. When the Polos' caravan arrived, Barka's tents were pitched at Sarai on the lower Volga, in the region of modern Astrakhan. All went smoothly. 'Barka received Messer Niccolò and Messer Maffeo with great honour and was very glad they had come.' The Polo brothers then pulled off a rapid piece of extremely profitable trading. They not only got a return of double the value of their trade jewels but extracted from Barka a trading concession within the Khan's territory which added even more to their profits. But twelve months of lucrative barter under the benevolent patronage of Barka Khan were brought to an abrupt and doubtless infuriating close by the outbreak of an all-out Tartar war – a war which sealed off the Polos from their homeland in the West, and whose effects led the brothers to the Court of Kubilai Khan.

Hulagu Khan feasts before leaving Mongolia to invade Persia. His great achievement was the subjugation of the Baghdad caliphate. (Asiatic Society of Bengal MS D31, f 120.)

This war is a significant milestone in the Tartar story, showing the western khanates coming to blows with all the pomp and ceremony of military empires. We are told that the war had its origins in a frontier dispute between Barka and Hulagu, and that it took six months for the two sides to raise their armies. When the war finally came, it developed into a struggle of attrition with the balance finally swinging in favour of Hulagu, but while it lasted it was impossible for the Polos to retrace their steps to Sudak. They therefore decided to make a wide detour to the east before making another attempt to get home.

The first concern of the Polos was, as might be expected, to get themselves and their goods well out of the war zone, and they accomplished this by pushing up the Volga river. They reached a city named Ucaca, which Marco rather confusingly calls 'the limit of the territory of the Western Khan', and which seems to have been in the region of Saratov. And from Ucaca they began their long march to the east and south, heading across arid steppe land sparsely populated by nomad Tartar communities, and through the land corridor which separates the Aral Sea from the Caspian.

After what was clearly an exhausting march, the Polos found temporary refuge and refreshment in the trade centre of Bukhara. But although the local ruler, Barak, was indifferent to the arrival of two more merchants in a city whose life was trade, Bukhara was still uncomfortably close to the frontiers of Hulagu Khan. The Polos found that they were no better off, for the war in the West was still raging. They could not go back; they could not go forward. And in Bukhara they stayed, as Marco baldly states, for three years. All we know of this hiatus in their lives is that they clearly made the best of a bad job. Certainly they expanded their working knowledge of the Tartar dialects into fluency. And in view of their trading skills it is hard to imagine them failing to add to their capital and overall profits. . . .

The marooned Polo brothers were abruptly rescued from their three-year sojourn in Bukhara by the arrival of a VIP emissary from Hulagu Khan in the West. Hulagu had despatched this worthy on a diplomatic mission to the Court of Kubilai Khan himself. Bukhara lay on the emissary's line of route; and in Bukhara he found the Polos. Perhaps the envoy was under orders to compile a dossier on the cities through which he travelled, which would account for the interview with the Polos which followed. The brothers would certainly have been brought to the notice of the Khan's emissary because of their curiosity value. From Marco's account two points of interest stand out. The Polos were the first Latins to visit the region in living memory (Bukhara is to the south of the route taken by Piano Carpini and Roubrouck). And Kubilai Khan, to use the words put into the envoy's mouth by Marco, 'had never seen any Latin and very much wanted to meet one'. Lured by the envoy's offer of guaranteed safe-conduct travel and a lucrative reception at the Great Khan's Court, the Polos set off on their travels again, their destination 'the ends of the earth': Cathay.

2 Mission

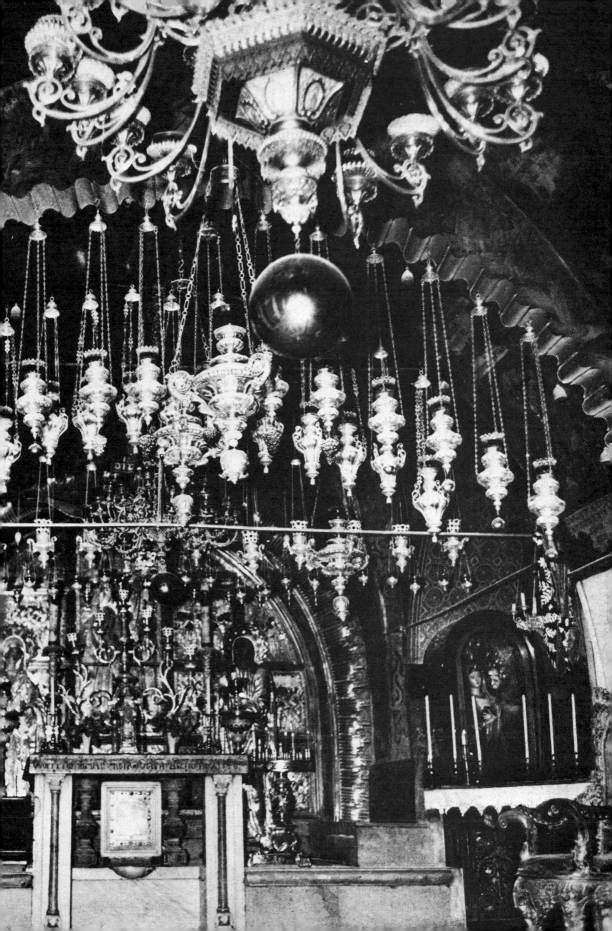

C ATHAY', THANKS TO THE STORIES which Marco brought back, became for over two centuries synonymous with Eldorado – a fabulous land of wealth on the far side of the world. Significantly, the word itself was Mongol-based, from *Khitai* – a nomad tribe which had wandered into northern China before the days of Jenghiz. For details of the journey there which the Polo brothers made on the advice of Hulagu's envoy, it is necessary to work backwards from Marco's account. He lays a deliberate 'cliff-hanger' for his readers, saying coyly 'Messer Marco, the son of Messer Niccolò, who saw all these things also, will tell you of them in plain terms further on in the book.' But he says enough to make it clear that the Great Khan's envoy had not been travelling at the breakneck pace which characterized top-priority business in the Mongol Empire. It took them a full year to get there.

The route which makes most sense for the Polos to have taken had three main legs. The first was straightforward enough: Bukhara/Samarkand/Kashgar. Then came the murderous obstacle of the Gobi Desert, a journey punctuated by the oases of Turfan and Hami. The party would then have headed south-east for Tun-huang, Suchow and Kanchow, which lie at the westernmost ex-tremity of the Great Wall of China – that colossal monument which had already proved as useless for keeping out invaders as Hadrian's Wall and the Maginot Line. Once the landmark of the Great Wall had been picked up, the last leg of the journey was easy: following the course of the Wall to the new capital of the Great Khan, Khanbalig – Mongol Peking.

So it was that for the first time Europeans looked on the For-bidden City as it was under Kubilai Khan. If Marco's reaction as recorded in the *Travels* is anything to go by, they marvelled at the serene lay-out of the city, with its chessboard pattern of streets surrounding the walled Imperial Palace at its core. The outer perimeter of the city was some twenty-four miles round, with defensive walls thirty feet high and as thick again at the foot. When the Polo brothers were led into the presence of the Great Khan, Kubilai 'received them honourably and welcomed them with lavish hospitality and was altogether delighted that they had come'. But after relishing the Great Khan's affable welcome and resting in long-unaccustomed luxury, the Polo brothers found themselves on the receiving end of a barrage of questions which went on for months.

First on the list, obviously, was a political description of Europe. Any ruler of Kubilai's status, questioning representatives

A portrait of Kubilai Khan, from a Chinese engraving: one of the illustrations used in Sir Henry Yule's *The Book of Ser Marco Polo*, 1875 edition.

from what amounted to another world, would have wanted to know if he had any direct counterpart there and, if not, who were the rulers who counted for anything. It would have been impossible for the Polos to have given a run-down of the rulers of Europe without mentioning the Papacy but the conversation would have got around to it anyway, for Kubilai was fascinated by religion. An open-minded realist who saw no faith as a threat to his own power, he wanted to know about them all, and this was his first contact with a couple of genuine Western Christians. It is impossible to think of Kubilai as a credulous barbarian clutching at spiritual lifebuoys. He seems to have been a cross between an amateur theologian and a very human character who relished the extraordinary – performers of the Indian rope-trick or conjurers who could send his drinking-cup floating through the air to his hand. Marco later recorded Kubilai's comparative disenchantment (though not any lessening of his tolerance) with Christianity, because Christians could not perform such sleight-of-hand 'miracles'. But Kubilai's first meeting with the Polos must have given him a definite respect for Christians: these were very tough men who obviously had a motivation quite as strong as that possessed by the Tartars themselves. And he wanted to know about it.

36

It was a very long session of question and answer: it lasted all of a year. But when the Polos finally obtained Kubilai's leave to go home, they found themselves, willy-nilly, entrusted with one of the most important missions in the history of Christendom: to escort a Tartar ambassador to the Pope himself. Kubilai was clearly motivated by his religious curiosity, but it is worth remembering that a mission to Rome was a very good way of opening up diplomatic channels in Europe without having to concentrate on any one country, and so getting bogged down in European power-struggles. Bearing in mind that the Polos were true sons of Venice, the state which had proved its mastery of the hard realities of international in-fighting, Kubilai was probably acting on the brothers' advice. It was exactly the sort of diplomatic overture which would have appealed to the toughest overlord wanting to open new avenues of possibility: an embassy with no commitments and all the goodwill in the world to be gained.

Marco chose to put an orthodox Christian interpretation on Kubilai's requirements from the Pope. The first of these was

up to a hundred men learned in the Christian religion, well versed in the seven arts and skilled to argue and demonstrate plainly to idolaters and those of other persuasions that their religion is utterly mistaken and that all the idols which they keep in their houses and worship are things of the Devil – men able to show by clear reasoning that the Christian religion is better than theirs.

This was a transparent twisting of the facts, the result of Marco's deep-rooted hero-worship of Kubilai, who had not been impressed by what he had seen of Christians who had come to China from Karakorum. It also contradicts what Marco himself later wrote of Kubilai's discussion with Niccolò and Maffeo about the Christian faith, which is far more revealing. Marco has Kubilai asking:

Why should I become a Christian? You can see for yourselves that the Christians who live in these parts are so ignorant that they cannot do anything, while these idolaters can do what they like. When I sit at table they can send the cups out in the middle of the hall, full of wine or anything else, straight to my hand without anyone touching them, when I wish to drink. They can send bad weather packing in any direction they choose. And as you know, their idols talk and tell them whatever they want to know. If I were to be converted to the faith of Christ and become a Christian, my barons and others who do not believe in Christ would ask me 'What are you thinking of, getting baptised and adopting the faith of Christ? Have you seen any virtues or miracles to his credit?'

It was an odd mixture of superstition and open-mindedness. Kubilai was obviously well-disposed towards what he had heard of Christianity. Yet as far as he was concerned, the proof of the spiritual pudding was a demonstrable 'miracle'. He was not merely asking for missionaries to spread the light, though they would be welcome, but men 'who will show their mastery by making the idolaters powerless to perform these marvels in their presence. On the day when we see this, I too will condemn them and their religion. Then I will be baptised, and all my barons and magnates will do likewise, and their subjects in turn will undergo baptism. So there will be more Christians here than there are in your part of the world.' For all the culture and free-thinking which Kubilai undoubtedly possessed, his 'show me' attitude was the reaction of any intelligent pagan in wanting to know the by-products of the Christian message.

This clearly inspired Kubilai's request for a sample of the oil that burned in the lamp of the Church of the Holy Sepulchre in Jerusalem. This is interesting on several counts. There is nothing in Marco's version to suggest that any mention was made of such traditional relics as a chip of the True Cross or a saint's toenail, and we would like to think that Kubilai was in fact offered such a relic but turned it down as being 'too obvious'. Perhaps, too, the Polos were slightly staggered by the amount of learned missionaries required by Kubilai – after all, a hundred doctors of divinity would have been more than several European universities of the time possessed between them – and suggested the oil in the belief that it would be more ~ceptable to the Pope. Another faint possibility is that the Polos were fishing for Tartar aid for the Latin kingdom of Jerusalem. They had certainly seen the power of Hulagu Khan at first hand, and may have tried to get Kubilai to put pressure on Hulagu for the latter to help Jerusalem.

This, then, was the mission which Kubilai asked Niccolò and Maffeo Polo to bring before the Pope. It was thoroughly official, with written credentials (in Turkish), and the man selected by Kubilai to be the first Tartar ambassador in the West was a baron by the name of Kogatai. He and the two Polos were given the Great Khan's passports throughout the Mongol dominions: tablets of gold twelve inches by three, engraved with the Great Khan's order to supply the bearer with all necessary food, shelter and transport animals on pain of death.

The mission set out from Khanbalig in the spring of 1266, retracing the course of the Polos' outward journey. It was beset

38

A Chinese drawing of a
typical Tartar noble
on horseback.

with acts of God, starting with the long illness of Baron Kogatai.
The Polos eventually left him and pushed on alone, relying on the
power of the Great Khan's passports. After reaching Bukhara, they
decided to head straight for the Mediterranean round the southern
toe of the Caspian, via Baghdad. They reached the north-eastern
extremity of the Mediterranean at Ayas and headed south to Acre,
where they arrived in April 1269. The return journey had taken
the Polos all of three years 'because they could not ride all the time,
but were delayed by bad weather, by snow and by swollen rivers'.

The return of the Polos coincided with an event which they had not bargained for: the death of a Pope and the ensuing vacancy of the Holy See. This was the discouraging news which greeted them at Ayas. But as events turned out, they saved themselves no little time by travelling to Acre, for there they found the Papal Legate Theobald, spiritual overlord of the Holy Land. Theobald welcomed the Polos' news with great enthusiasm and backed them whole-heartedly, but at the time the soundest advice he could give them was to wait until a new Pope was elected. Niccolò and Maffeo knew very well that they could hardly convey Kubilai's message to a lesser dignitary of the Church without causing possible offence, but they would have been less than human if they had not leaped at the chance to go home to Venice in the meantime. Sad news was waiting for Niccolò when he got home: his wife had died. But he was certainly comforted and impressed by his son Marco, now grown into an energetic and intelligent fifteen-year-old.

Two years passed while dissension raged in the Papal Curia at Rome and the Polos chafed in Venice. Then Niccolò and Maffeo decided that they dare wait no longer to fulfil the Great Khan's mission. Their plan was to head first for Acre, there to talk matters over with the Legate Theobald, and they sailed from Venice – taking Marco with them. It is not hard to imagine the boy begging to go: anyone in his place and of his age, having drunk in stories about a wonderful new world for over two years, would have wanted to go there with the father and uncle who had gone before him and returned safely. Niccolò must also have reflected that the long and unaccustomed sea trip from Venice to Acre would probably be more than sufficient to test Marco's endurance. If he had had enough by the time they got to the Holy Land, no matter: he could always be put on a boat home.

Further intense discussions with Theobald ensued at Acre. The papal election seemed to be as far as ever from reaching a definite result, and Theobald agreed that the Great Khan could not be kept waiting much longer. One part of the mission could be fulfilled at once: the obtaining of a sample of the holy oil from Jerusalem, and the Polos set off with Theobald's approval and, presumably, his written authorization. When they got back to Acre with the oil, Theobald had no more positive news for them and Niccolò made the decision to go. Theobald provided the party with a letter to Kubilai testifying that the Polos had done everything in their power, considering the very difficult situation, to carry out Kubilai's wishes; and Niccolò, Maffeo and Marco left Acre for

OPPOSITE A thirteenth-century mosaic at St Mark's, Venice, showing the Doge and clergy at prayer.

41

Pope Gregory x. This wise
and zealous pope had an
inspired conception of the
role of the Papacy. He
strove for peace in Europe
and union of the Roman and
Greek Churches, as well
as the defence of the Latin
Kingdom of Jerusalem.

Ayas to start the overland journey to China.

Then events seemed to intervene at the eleventh hour and smile
on the mission. The Polos were overtaken at Ayas with dramatic
news. At last, there was a new Pope – none other than Theobald,
who had assumed the name of Pope Gregory x of Piacenza. The
message summoned the Polos, assuming that they could still be
reached, to the papal presence, and they immediately took ship for
Acre.

The new Pope Gregory's enthusiasm for the mission proved as
deep as ever. He could not provide a hundred priests of the calibre

The Piazzetta at Venice: an engraving from *The Book of Ser Marco Polo*.

required by Kubilai, but he put the two leading friars in the Holy Land at the disposal of the mission. Both were Dominicans: Brother Nicholas of Vicenza and Brother William of Tripoli. Gregory gave the friars extraordinary powers of ordination and the granting of absolution: they were to be true papal viceroys in the realms of the Great Khan. He sent a personal message to Kubilai as well as costly gifts, which Marco dismisses with unusual vagueness as 'fine vessels of crystal and other things'. In addition, Gregory made the first positive move towards establishing a diplomatic *entente* between the Christian West and the Mongol Empire. This took the

form of a letter to Barka Khan of the Golden Horde, asking that
Christians might be given 'aid and favour' so that they could travel
in his dominions.

At last, five years after Niccolò and Maffeo had set out from
Khanbalig, it seemed that the mission was a going concern.
Kubilai's expressions of goodwill had been reciprocated in the
fullest measure by Pope Gregory. The men intended to found the
greatest province of the Christian Church ever created had been

44

Marco Polo sets off from Venice with his father and his uncle in 1271, at the start of their second journey. From *Le Livre des Merveilles*. This late-fourteenth-century illuminated manuscript described the journeys of travellers such as Sir John Mandeville, and his predecessors Marco Polo and Roubrouck.

assigned their duties. With the glowing satisfaction that everything possible had been done to achieve success, the Polos' mission to Cathay set out from Acre with the blessing of the Pope.

Seldom can such justified hopes have been dashed so quickly.

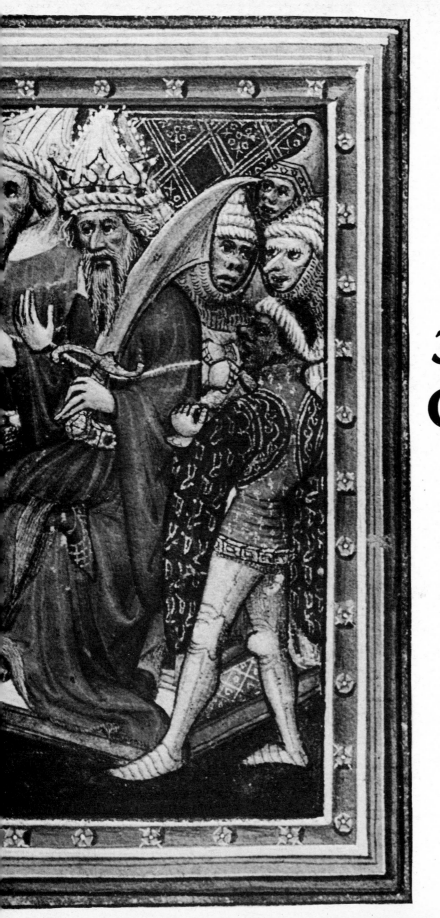

3
Crisis

FOR NICCOLÒ AND MAFFEO, the blow of fate which beset their second journey at its outset must have been depressingly reminiscent of their first trip. Just when things seemed to be going really well, the brothers were caught up in a war which had nothing to do with them and which seemed to wreck their prospects. This time, however, it was not a Tartar war which was to blame, but a long-range extension of the military prowess of Mamluk Egypt.

Ever since throwing Hulagu Khan's army out of Egypt after Ain Jalut in 1260, the Mamluks had shown that they owned military talents worthy of the Tartars themselves. Long-range raiding in force was the Mamluks' forte. The victor of Ain Jalut, Sultan Bibars, had developed as a feared and famed warlord. His charisma may be judged by his boast that he had played tennis in Cairo and Damascus in the same week. In the eleven years since Ain Jalut, Mamluk energy had converted Palestine and Syria into a no-man's-land in which the initiative had been relinquished by the Tartar ilkhanate of Persia – Hulagu Khan's effective western frontier seems to have been the natural delineation of the Euphrates river. Judging by the silence of Marco's account, Niccolò and Maffeo encountered no trouble from the Mamluks in the last leg of their journey across Mesopotamia and through Syria to the Mediterranean. But now, in 1271, the Mamluks blocked the Polos with a vengeance. When the mission arrived at Ayas for the first stage of its journey east – through Christian Armenia to upper Mesopotamia – it was greeted with the news that the entire hinterland was being terrorized by Mamluk raiders under a leader whom Marco identifies as Bundukdari, Sultan of Egypt, who 'came into Armenia with a great host and wrought great havoc in the country, and the missionaries went in peril of their lives'.

We can sympathize with the new Pope's nominees for the mission, poor Brother William and Brother Nicholas. Until very recently they had been leading secure and prestigious careers under Theobald's wing. Then they had been given the daunting task of converting an unknown empire which was apparently the greatest in the world, yet so far away that no one had ever heard of it. At least they had been given competent guides who had actually been to the new world and had got back in one piece. But this was something completely unlooked-for: mortal danger before so much as a single day's march had been made inland from the Mediterranean, a peril from which not even the tough and experienced Polo brothers could see any way out. The missionary zeal of

PREVIOUS PAGES 'The Christians are alarmed at the Caliph's words': the Caliph of Baghdad demanded from them a miracle that would prove the Christian faith, and according to legend they produced one. An illustration from *Les Livres du Graunt Caam* (f 222v) giving a very European view of the Khan's Court and Marco Polo's experiences there.

OPPOSITE The medieval citadel of Aleppo in Syria. This fell to the Mongols in 1260. However, the Mamluks were able to prevent their further advance into Egypt.

Travellers in Armenia: Marco encountered
many such traders during the outward
journey through the Middle East.
From *Le Livre des Merveilles*.

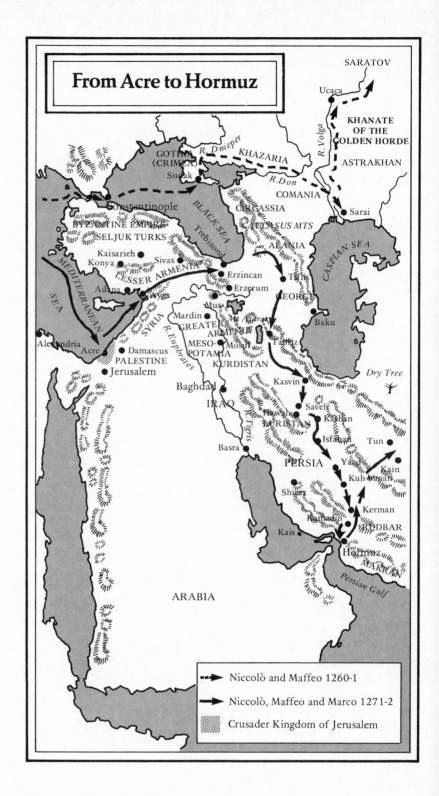

From Acre to Hormuz

SARATOV

Ucaca

KHANATE OF THE GOLDEN HORDE

ASTRAKHAN

R. Volga

GOTHIA (CRIMEA)

Sudak

R. Dnieper

KHAZARIA

R. Don

COMANIA

Sarai

BLACK SEA

Constantinople

BYZANTINE EMPIRE

SELJUK TURKS

CIRCASSIA

CAUCASUS MTS

ALANIA

Trebizond

Kaisarieh

Sivas

Konya

LESSER ARMENIA

Erzincan

Erzerum

Tiflis

GEORGIA

CASPIAN SEA

Baku

Adana

MEDITERRANEAN SEA

Mardin

Mush

Mt Ararat

GREATER ARMENIA

MESO-POTAMIA

Mosul

Tabriz

SYRIA

R. Euphrates

KURDISTAN

Dry Tree

Alexandria

Acre

Damascus

PALESTINE

Jerusalem

Baghdad

Kasvin

IRAQ

R. Tigris

LURISTAN

Saveh

Kashan

Basra

Isfahan

Tun

PERSIA

Yazd

Kain

Kuh-banan

Shiraz

Kerman

Kamadin

RODBAR

Kais

Hormuz

MAKRAN

Persian Gulf

ARABIA

- - -► Niccolò and Maffeo 1260-1

——► Niccolò, Maffeo and Marco 1271-2

▦ Crusader Kingdom of Jerusalem

the two friars evaporated: let alone go any further, they would return to Acre. And they did, leaving the mission high and dry without its professional missionaries.

One can only imagine the bitterness which must have touched Niccolò and Maffeo Polo at this moment. They had stood in the presence of the Great Khan and had heard him express his queries and doubts about the bed-rock of the Christian faith. The Polos had done their best as Christians and Europeans, promising to bring Kubilai the proof of their asseverations. And now, they must have reflected, how could they go back and face him? The mere presence of danger had caused the Pope's chosen representatives to turn tail and run at the outset of their mission. 'Loss of face' is an Oriental characteristic which the brothers would already have encountered in their travels in the Far East, but not wanting to look a fool is a universal human emotion. The desertion of the friars – and its implications – must have shaken both the religious faith and the human confidence of the Polos to an extent which we can still sense today.

From the depths of disappointment there re-emerged the brothers' courageous decision to go back to Cathay empty-handed and explain their failure to Kubilai face to face. By now any doubts about young Marco's staying-power seem to have been firmly dispelled and he was one of the party. And his eager eye for fine cities and scenery, together with any interesting facts and stories connected with them, was later transcribed from memory and immortalized in his personal account of the Polos' odyssey.

Some comment on the content of Marco's *Travels* is necessary here. It is not a blow-by-blow itinerary. The main cities in his line of route are described in detail, but so are others in the neighbourhood. Marco was trying to give the clearest possible picture of the countries through which he had travelled, not merely to tell the story of 'one man's journey to the ends of the earth'. His account is as appealing as it is because it radiates enthusiasm and energy – but neither of these attributes is a cast-iron guarantee of accuracy. What we have is a wide-ranging travelogue with a central spine: the actual route along which Marco journeyed. The Prologue gives only the sketchiest *précis* of the Polos' two trips to Cathay, and Marco's main account is almost entirely devoid of motives for any incidental changes of route. In later life Marco chafed because so many people took his stories with a grain of salt; but more detail in his travels about himself, his father and his uncle would have spared posterity a lot of vituperative guesswork, however intelligent.

53

Thus, after telling us that the papal mission fell apart because of the terror inspired by Sultan Bundukdari and his Mamluk hordes, Marco makes no further mention of them but turns to his description of the cities and terrain of Armenia, the first stage of the journey. It is left to his readers to deduce that Niccolò and Maffeo decided to repeat the manœuvre by which they had got away from the war between Barka Khan and Hulagu Khan ten years before: a wide swing to the north. This took the party first to the southern Caucasus and the kingdom of Georgia, then south parallel with the western shore of the Caspian Sea and finally into western Persia, safe in undisputed Tartar territory. This was a big detour which skirted northern Mesopotamia, where Bundukdari's raiders seem to have been concentrating their efforts. And enduring pangs of bitterness caused by the flight of the friars were certainly heightened by the fact that the detour saved the travellers from any molestation by the Mamluks. Thanks to the successful evasive tactics adopted by Niccolò and Maffeo, the danger which had seemed so terrifying at Ayas never materialized at all.

Marco's description of the trip through 'Lesser Armenia' (the coastal region immediately inland from Ayas) and 'Greater Armenia' (between the Caucasus and upper Mesopotamia) sets the style for the entire narrative of the *Travels*. The country was Christian and tributary to the Tartars, who tolerated religious preferences on the part of their subjects as long as the latter paid up with their taxes. Marco mentions the key cities of Turkey to the north-west (Konya, Kaisarieh and Sivas) and those to the south-east (Mus, Mardin, Mosul, Tabriz and Bayburt with its silver mine). Major landmarks for the Polos started with the city of Erzincan, 'in which is made the finest buckram in the world and countless other crafts are practised. Here are the finest baths of spring water to be found anywhere on earth.' These superlatives are a classic example of Marco's over-reaction to excellence, and help us to understand why he ended his life with the nickname of 'Marco Millions'. Then Mount Ararat, on which the Ark was said to have grounded and was rumoured to be still visible, given the right conditions, in Marco's time, naturally gets a paragraph to itself in the *Travels*.

From Mount Ararat, with its Biblical associations and local legends, Marco turns east with an interesting reference to the famous oilfield of Baku on the western Caspian – a reference in which oil is given considerably more homely values than those which appeal in the oil-crazy twentieth century. 'This oil is not good to eat,' notes Marco solemnly; 'but it is good for burning and as a salve for men and camels afflicted with itch or scab. Men come from a long distance to fetch this oil, and in all the neighbourhood no other oil is burned but this.' It is curious to think of camels and mules plying as primitive oil tankers; Marco's interest in the phenomenon was probably aroused by being held up on the road by a caravan loaded with odd-looking panniers, smelly and leaking.

One of Marco's reactions to the approaches to Georgia was to note the mountain defences, which have proved too much of an obstacle to invaders through the centuries; and as token of this he quotes the frustration of Alexander the Great and of the Tartars themselves. 'The whole country is full of high mountains and narrow passes which are easily defensible, so that I can assure you that the Tartars have never been able to achieve complete dominion over it.' But Marco, for all that he possessed a good eye for terrain, was no military cartographer; the mercantile stamp of his family upbringing always shows through clearly and takes the lead. 'The province has villages and towns in plenty. Silk is produced here in abundance, and the silken fabrics and cloth-of-gold woven here are the finest ever seen. There are also the best goshawks in the world. There are ample supplies of everything, and commerce and industry flourish.' At times, bazaar cries and fast sales-talk – 'best silk', 'best cloth-of-gold', 'best goshawks' – seem to rub off on Marco's style in a manner which seems less than businesslike, for all that he was obviously impressed with the goods. To Georgia's metropolis, Tiflis (still, under the name of Tbilisi, the capital of the Georgian Soviet Socialist Republic today), Marco gives his standard 'four-star' rating of 'a fine city of great size'.

We can pinpoint Tiflis as the 'farthest north' of the Polos' detour, if only because Marco's interest subsequently turns inexorably to the south. It is a wistful sequence because it covers Mesopotamia, which Marco had clearly set his heart on seeing but had been prevented from doing so because of the Mamluk irruption. He was clearly fascinated by the vanished supremacy of the Caliphs of Baghdad, which Hulagu Khan's armies had pounded into the dust. Marco tells of the momentous doings when Baghdad fell and Hulagu confronted the captured caliph with his now-useless treasure hoard. 'Why did you not take your treasure and give it to knights and hired soldiers to defend you and your city?' With Tartar ingenuity and cruelty, Hulagu ordered the treasure to be dumped in a tower and the caliph to be locked in with it. 'Now, Caliph, eat your treasure, since you are so fond of it; for you will get nothing else.' It took the wretched man four days to die. 'So it would have been better indeed for the Caliph', is Marco's sententious comment, 'if he had given away his treasure to defend his land and his people rather than died with all his people and bereft of everything.'

This cautionary tale, which must have been a classic in Tartar legend, is followed immediately in the *Travels* by the story of a miracle. Dwelling on the former power of the Caliphs of Baghdad, Marco tells of the caliph who threatened a massacre of Christians unless they could produce a miracle for him. This was the assertion that a Christian with enough faith 'the size of a grain of mustard-seed' could cause a mountain to move; and he gave a trembling deputation of local Christians ten days to do just that. With black humour, the story tells of the Christians' frantic search for a man of sufficient virtue. This worthy was finally run to earth in the form of a cobbler who was so holy that he had put out one of his own eyes with a bradawl for looking with excessive relish on the foot and leg of an attractive lady customer. Despite his protests the cobbler was persuaded to pray, and the mountain moved, saving the Christians.

There are obvious reasons for the length at which Marco spins out the story, the clearest being the contrast between the vanished power of the caliphs and the summary treatment which Hulagu dealt out to the last of them. But it is possible that Marco lumped the two stories into a single passage of his narrative because they had occurred that way in a discussion with Kubilai Khan, and that the exchange had stuck in his mind. Why should they not have done so? The capture of Baghdad was a major milestone in the Tartar story; the fall of the caliphs was an obvious indication that the Moslem faith had serious limitations, whereas the Christian miracle which had prevailed over that astonished caliph was just the kind of story which would have interested Kubilai. We can imagine Marco using it in an attempt to bolster Kubilai's attitude to Christianity – although we can almost hear Kubilai pointing out that even if a moving mountain was much more impressive than flying drinking-cups, he had yet to see it for himself. . . .

Although the two stories form an emphatic interlude in Marco's account, his treatment of Mesopotamia is a good example of his 'long-range' coverage of places not directly on the beaten track. First, the kingdom of Mosul, and again the professional mercantile

OPPOSITE A modern view of the 'Golden Friday' Mosque, the palace of Harun al-Rashid, Caliph of Baghdad and contemporary of Charlemagne. He featured in some of the stories of the *Arabian Nights*.

56

touch. 'Here are made all the cloths of silk and gold called *mosulin*. And from this kingdom hail the great merchants, also called "Mosulin", who export vast quan' 'es of spices and other precious wares.' Next come Mus and Mardin with their cotton and buckram, and then Baghdad, with its pearls, fabric and academic fame. 'It is a great centre for the study of the law of Mahomet and of necromancy, natural science, astronomy, geomancy and physiognomy. It is the largest and most splendid city in all these parts.' From Baghdad itself Marco mentions the eighteen-day journey needed to travel down the Tigris to the Persian Gulf (which he calls the 'Indian Sea'). Basra features prominently – 'in groves all around Basra grow the best dates in the world'.

All this detail about Mesopotamia can be – and indeed has been – taken to mean that the Polos did indeed travel down-river to the Persian Gulf after quitting Georgia. But this would have taken them far from the places subsequently mentioned and there is no mention of sea travel to the next major milestone on the journey out to Cathay: Hormuz. On the other hand, there is a definite feeling of getting back to the subject in the way in which Marco tears himself away from talking about Baghdad and Basra, Hulagu and the caliph, the miracle of the praying cobbler, etc, etc, and suddenly starts describing the city of Tabriz in Persia.

Now Tabriz, and the cities in the order that Marco goes on to describe, lie on a much more easterly route which ends on the Persian Gulf at Hormuz. And there would appear to be little reason for the Polos, having successfully evaded the Mamluks by their march to Georgia, to have swung back to the west before pressing on with their journey eastwards. Marco points out that Tabriz is a mercantile crossroads, doing much business with India, Baghdad, Mosul and Hormuz. 'Many Latin merchants come here to buy the merchandise imported from foreign lands. It is also a market for precious stones, which are found here in great abundance. It is a city where good profits are made by travelling merchants' – Niccolò and Maffeo, seasoned old traffickers that they were, must have wished they could have stayed.

Tabriz is Marco's basis for a brief description of the provinces of Tartar Persia, and first on his list is the town of Saveh, with the ornate tombs containing the preserved bodies of the three Magi (Gaspar, Melchior and Balthasar) who visited the infant Christ in Bethlehem. Deeply impressed by these shrines, Marco goes on to tell of the local legend connected with the Magi. The Christ child's parting gift to them was a small casket, which they opened in

curiosity on the journey home. All they found was a small stone, which they threw down a well in disappointment. At once the well burst into miraculous flame, kept burning ever since – the basis of Persian fire-worship, an explanation which puts a thirteenth-century Christian interpretation on the ancient cult of Zoroaster.

Marco concludes with the statement that the three Magi came from Saveh, Hawah and Kashan, and taken in that order these three towns lie directly on the road the Polos took to Hormuz. After Saveh and its wondrous tombs, Marco describes no city between Saveh and Yazd, which is also on the route; but he tells of the local horseflesh and the danger of bandits. He has particular admiration for the local asses, 'sold for fully two hundred pounds of Touraine apiece'. Although the Polos certainly saw the virtues of these asses at first hand, there is a slightly rueful note in the references to their price. 'This is because they eat little, carry heavy loads and travel long distances in a single day, enduring toil beyond the power of horses or mules.'

Marco Polo hears the story of the three kings. According to Marco's account, each king visited Christ separately, the youngest first, and it seemed to each that he was of their own age and size. However, when they went back together, he appeared to them as a baby. The illustration is from *Les Livres du Graunt Caam* (f 223v).

59

A wild ass from Mongolia:
from *The Book of Ser
Marco Polo*.

To men uniquely concerned with mileage and staying-power,
the importance of such qualities was obvious:

Here merchants travelling from one country to another have to cope
with extensive deserts: dry, barren, sandy regions where no grass or
fodder suitable for horses is to be found. Freshwater wells and springs
lie so far apart that travellers must make long marches if their beasts are
to get anything to drink. Since horses cannot endure such conditions
the merchants prefer these asses, which are fast, steady and cheaper to
keep. So they fetch a better price than horses.

The local horses and asses were an important export, finding
ready markets in India; and on the latter point Marco includes a
weird superstition of the day: 'Note that in India the climate is so
hot that horses cannot be bred and are not born, or, if they are,
they are monstrosities, blemished and misshapen in their limbs,
and quite worthless.'

Well-mounted though they were while travelling through Persia,
the Polos had to cope with the problem of the local bandits. The
Tartar régime had been unable to root out the bandits. Instead,
like a harassed wartime admiralty, it had instituted a convoy

60

system. 'Along all dangerous routes the inhabitants at the request of the merchants shall supply good and efficient escorts from district to district for their safe conduct on payment of two or three groats for each loaded beast according to the length of the journey.' This arrangement would have been wide open to local corruption – it is easy to imagine the roaring trade which a professional escort-furnisher could have made, first charging exorbitant protection-money from caravans and then tipping off the bandits on where and when to attack, and splitting the loot with them. Marco states that the system did not in fact work very well: 'these brigands are not to be deterred from frequent depredations. Unless merchants are well armed and equipped with bows, they slay and harry them unsparingly.' This conjures up a picture of the party on their tough donkeys, ambling along in a caravan of nervous traders, armed to the teeth and keeping a constant eye on the hills.

A scathing note on Moslem morals is added by Marco: the locals drink wine, forbidden by Islamic law, and are hypocrites to boot. 'They gloss the text of their law thus: if wine is boiled over a fire, so that it is partly consumed and turns sweet, they are free to drink it without breaking commandment or law; for they no longer call it wine, since the change of flavour carries with it a change of name.'

The next checkpoint to be identified is the city of Yazd with its silken fabric – the principal export; and then, after seven more days of rough-riding in which the traveller must cover 'a plain in which there are only three inhabited places where he can get shelter', Marco describes the city-state of Kerman, which was to be an important landmark on the Polos' journey. When Marco saw it, Kerman was a puppet-state, with its lordship granted at the pleasure of the Tartar overlord. One of Kerman's most important assets was turquoise-mining. Falconry was another booming market: 'in the mountains hereabouts are bred the best falcons in the world, and the swiftest . . . there is no bird that can escape from them by flight' – which makes the cynical reader wonder what had happened to the superb goshawks of Georgia!

Marco then strikes a somewhat contradictory note by relating a charming story: after describing the excellence and skill of the craftsmen of Kerman in making every conceivable item of war-gear from armour to spurs, he tells of the ruler of Kerman who worried about violence. The ruler noted that although Kerman itself was relatively peaceful, the neighbouring kingdoms were

61

Two nomad travellers in conversation. Such travellers went in constant danger to life and limb from bandits, and sometimes hired local inhabitants to guard and guide them.

OPPOSITE Mongol warriors besiege a city. From the *Jami al-tavarikh.*

باغی شده ولب خود توک کنگ واک کرده معنی آن زبان ختای سلطان ملکی اند وار همه قضا ازان واقع شده که حینک
دلایت ختای ویر او را منع کرده وبازکشت وایان خان بغرا ربای بود واحوا وطی سرد شده که می زمت آب وکا هم ان حاجب
بشره ما لک در ولایت مانده حالی مانده ما سعد ملول طوایف هراسری حوشین راحاکم وسلطان ملکی می ساخت وبعد ازان مدع
برج ذرا با امرا فوکنگ وسنجو کنگ محا وظت شهرحاکم رود احاک رود بربهرها موز مرد دنت میکشنگ حنک
هادی را حمیوت دنیک ارقوم حروج آمد شده بود دست کشه از مغول لزستاد نا ازصد و دلا کند ملک زند وان لشگر نه
ان الان خان کبخت البی فرستاد ه بودند از شجو کند ولشکر که ابخذ ملک ایان برنه و ان لشکر را با رود وند دبا سان نه
کردند

والان خان حون سنت ردار حالت بینشینه بود ده شهر حرنگ ونعار لنگ ومون لنگ ورعا بامانده امیرتوان روکسای نام بابه امیردیک
درسم کام سای دری فنیک فرستاده نماعا وحورش شهر حاک ما ورنه دبا سای کرده که ختای آرا سیم کوبند ومردا
کتای حوشین برد ارد حون بامانا رها شده انک تای ماه شهر وتلعه سور حوسیای زننه در کبار امرا با مانه
آلماک ببکشنگ حسکر حان با باما ن امانه اند دهر اینه امیرتوان هردوز مم می آورد ازیان با زرنه حون بنا
مل آنحا از نگای از دستکی که منت آدمی حرزده اندومی مرده ومونک حناک که الان اورا بسه جانه کند
آه شده وایه دبگرن وصیت او ناک نام حریک داشته وبخه در ولایت منگ ایان خان رنه وان

Tabriz, c.1360: a giraffe, its keeper and two other figures. From a contemporary Persian manuscript. Marco Polo described it as a city surrounded by beautiful gardens. The merchants there were wealthy but the inhabitants were mostly poor.

bywords for brawling, fighting and incidental mayhem. It must be the soil, decided his wise men. So the king sent for samples of the local soil from the neighbour-states – a total of seven ship-loads, which was then spread over the floor of banquet chambers and covered with carpets. The king then gave a banquet 'at which the guests had no sooner partaken of food than one began to round on another with opprobrious words and actions that soon led to blows. So the king agreed that the cause did indeed lie in the soil.'

We can safely imagine the Polos taking a brief rest at Kerman after their tough and dangerous ride from Tabriz; taking a generous estimate of their mileage as twenty miles a day, it must have taken them a month and a half. And Marco's coverage of Kerman in the *Travels* is a key point in his story as far as we are concerned. The Polos' journey there makes it obvious that they were making for Hormuz and had therefore decided to make at least part of their journey to Cathay by sea. This is remarkable in that neither

Niccolò nor Maffeo had had any direct experience of the Hormuz/India/Cathay sealane. They were clearly obsessed with making up the time lost while waiting around in Venice for a new Pope to be elected. Returning across Mesopotamia after their first journey, they would have heard about Basra and the port, Kais, from which ships sailed east; they would also have heard about Hormuz. For anyone contemplating a long sea voyage east, these would have been the two obvious destinations for an overland journey from the Mediterranean.

This in turn means that at some stage Marco sat in on a debate between Niccolò and Maffeo as to which port to choose. Hence his discussion of the Tigris route and the cities they would pass through if they took it. The elder Polos would have taken into account that if the Mamluks could put Christian Armenia in jeopardy, they could do precisely the same with Mesopotamia, and the logical decision to head further east would follow. Once they had arrived at Saveh after their journey Ayas/Erzincan/Tiflis/Tabriz, they could have swung east out of Persia, picking up the route along which they had returned from Cathay. But when they made the decision to push on to Yazd and Kerman, they must still have been intending to go on down to the coast at Hormuz and take ship for the east. The initial crisis was over; the long, evasive detour was completed; another gamble lay ahead, as great as but no less insuperable than any they had survived so far.

And at Kerman we can picture Marco, a tough and sunburned eighteen-year-old; hardened to the saddle and the privations of long desert marches and with the smattering of scores of minor dialects already at his command. His performance so far would have been a tremendous source of strength and encouragement to his father and uncle. Together the three of them now turned their faces to the sea.

4 To Hormuz

WHEN THE POLOS finally left Kerman, their road lay downhill through the country of Rudbar, which shelved down to the coast of the Persian Gulf at Hormuz. From that time, in Marco's account, one word begins to sound a *leit-motif* in the *Travels*: the heat.

A two-day descent from the Kerman uplands took the Polos on to the plain of Kamadin, where Marco first saw the striking hump-backed cattle of the region so strange to Western eyes. Another comparative oddity was the sheep: 'as big as asses, with tails so thick and plump that they weigh a good thirty pounds'. But soon the Polos had distractions other than the local fauna. They were entering one of the most dangerous regions they had yet encountered, a land oppressed and helpless under the constant menace of a brigand people: the Karaunas.

'Karaunas', Marco tells us, means 'mongrels' – the half-caste offspring of Indian mothers and Tartar fathers. The story of their origins, if Marco's account is correct, reminds us of how the African Matabele came into being in the nineteenth century, breaking away from the Zulu Empire under a rebel commander with his own armed following. Nigudar was the Karauna leader, and he was a nephew of the Great Khan himself. Nigudar gained territory for himself in northern India, warring on his Tartar neighbours with a private army over ten thousand strong and paying tribute to no man. The land of Rudbar was their favourite hunting-ground, for all that it was forty days' ride from their base, 'because in the winter all the merchants who come to do business in Hormuz, while they are awaiting the arrival of the merchants from India, send their mules and camels, which have grown thin with the long journey, to the plain of Rudbar to fatten on the rich pasturage, and here the Karaunas are on the look-out to seize them'.

Hard-headed observer though he was, Marco was as credulous as any European of his age, and he soberly affirms that the Karaunas had the power of raising a magic fog when they raided, attacking while their victims were frightened and confused by the choking gloom. This 'magic fog' has been explained away as 'dry fog': fine dust particles stirred up by the hot winds of the area, and a frightening phenomenon whose real cause had not been identified in Marco's time. Marco himself had very good reason to remember the Karaunas and their diabolical mist, for in one of the very few mentions of himself during the outward journey, he says that he experienced both but managed to escape to one of the fortified towns of the Rudbar plain.

PREVIOUS PAGES Camel caravans transport wood from the forested north of Mongolia to the Gobi Desert.

68

The whole episode is covered by two laconic sentences in the *Travels*, but it was obviously a narrow and dramatic escape. We can see the Polos' caravan winding across the Rudbar plain, and imagine the growing discomfort and uneasiness of the men in the column as the heat grew ever more unbearable and the dust-haze deepened, rising and reddening the sun to a dim copper blur. Then, out of the gloom, the sudden, unnerving attack. The column, doubtless already badly put out of joint by the descent of the dust-fog, broke in panic. Fast and instant flight was the only chance of survival, and this was just what the three Polos took. Emerging from the fringe of the fog at full gallop, they were spotted by the attackers, and a chase began, with the fugitives making for the nearest town. 'In this plain', notes Marco, 'there are many towns and villages with earthern walls of great height and thickness to protect them', and it was towards one of them, named 'Kamasal', that the Polos fled, beating their pursuers to the safety of the walls by a short head. The baffled Karaunas would have wasted no time in heading back to the shattered caravan for easier pickings before all the likely loot was gone.

After such a close escape the Polos must have waited for the next caravan, although Marco drops back into his 'Baedeker' style and makes no further reference to the incident and its aftermath. Nor can we doubt that when they did leave the safety of Kamasal, they wasted no time in pushing on to Hormuz. Marco estimates the journey as two days to cross the Rudbar plain, then a twenty-mile descent to the plain of Hormuz itself and a final two days to reach Hormuz.

Marco's memories of Hormuz are comparatively disjointed and dominated by the heat.

An excellent harbour . . . merchants come here by ship from India . . . the climate is torrid, owing to the heat of the sun, and unhealthy . . . the natives do not eat our sort of food . . . their ships are very bad . . . they have no iron for nails . . . the people . . . in summer do not stay in the cities or they would all die of the heat . . . several times in the summer . . . a wind so overpoweringly hot that it would be deadly . . . they plunge neck-deep into the water and so escape from the heat . . . all their fruits . . . ripened and done with by March . . . no vegetation anywhere except date-palms, which last till May. This is due to the great heat, which shrivels up everything.

As if he were unsure of conveying a sufficiently exhausting impression of the torrid atmosphere of Hormuz, Marco deliberately

Bandits attacking and
robbing passing travellers.
The Polos had to contend
with the Karaunas after
leaving Kerman. From
Le Livre des Merveilles.

punctuates his account with the grim story of an army of 6,600 foot and horse which marched against Hormuz from Kerman and made the mistake of bivouacking on the open plain near Hormuz during the night. When morning came, not a man nor a beast was still alive: the army had been blasted where it lay by the terrible hot wind. A final ghoulish touch: when the men of Hormuz went out to bury the corpses of their would-be conquerors, they could not move the bodies to the graves they had dug: 'they were so parched by the tremendous heat that the arms came loose from the trunk, so that there was nothing for it but to dig the graves beside the corpses and tip them in'.

After the ever-present heat, Marco turns to the main reason for the party's journey to Hormuz: its role as a centre of seaborne trade with the Far East. The Polos, as was only to be expected of Venetians to whom seafaring was a way of life, must have been appalled at the lemming-like attitude of the men of Hormuz towards sea travel. The ships were bad enough, as Marco makes clear. The hulls, with their wooden pegs and coconut-husk stitching, were undecked and relied on one mast, one sail and one rudder. Nor were the flexible seams efficiently caulked with pitch; they were smeared over with reeking fish-oil. Marco concedes one point: surprisingly enough, the stitching did stand up very well to salt water. But the overall performance of these gimcrack apologies for ships 'makes it a risky undertaking to sail in these ships. And you can take my word that many of them sink, because the Indian Ocean is often very stormy.'

The fear of taking risks was by this time, as we have seen, the very last charge which could be laid at the Polos' door. Nor were they averse to accepting a temporary setback and waiting until events made it possible for them to go on. But a detailed inspection of the ships in Hormuz harbour obviously proved too much for experienced travellers by land and sea who knew their business. They would have grown weary of hearing captain after voluble captain explain how many times they had made the journey to India. They had the evidence of their own eyes and accepted that there was no reasonable chance of their reaching India by sea from Hormuz.

While they were reluctantly coming to this depressing conclusion, they cannot have been cheered by the funereal atmosphere of the place. The word is meant literally: Marco includes a bitter paragraph about the mourning which was a speciality of the citizens of Hormuz. A four-year period was the norm for gentlewomen, and 'at least once a day', as Marco puts it, 'they assemble with their kinsfolk and neighbours and give themselves up to loud wailing and keening and lamenting the dead. Since deaths are frequent, they are never done with mourning.' It must all have come close to driving the Polos out of their minds.

Faced with this situation – the most daunting since the desertion of the friars back at Ayas – the Polos deliberated anew. Their decision was to scrap the original plan of a seaborne approach to the Far East and tackle the long overland route, starting by retracing their steps to the 'crossroads' of Kerman, where they could turn north-eastwards towards Turkestan.

Luck favoured them as they trekked back across Rudbar: they had no further trouble from the Karaunas, who had presumably started back to their lair in India with the spoils of their raid. And on leaving Kerman for the second time, the Polos got a vivid hint of the hardships which lay ahead in the form of a seven-day march through a desert. What water was to be found here was unbearably brackish; if drunk, it produced violent diarrhoea in man and beast. After this week of parched misery, abundant fresh water was encountered in the form of a copious spring, which was fortunate, for another four-day ordeal separated the travellers from the city of Kuh-banan, outside the kingdom of Kerman.

A stay at Kuh-banan would have been essential to recover and prepare for yet another thirsty march: eight days this time, according to Marco's reckoning, which took the Polos to the province named after the cities of Tun and Kain in the north of Persia. Here stood one of the oddest natural landmarks in the Mongol Empire, the Solitary or Dry Tree. This vast tree stood alone on a plain with no rivals for ten miles; it was believed that it marked the spot of the battle in which Alexander the Great smashed the last army of Darius of Persia. Marco records that this region was fertile and enjoyed a temperate climate, with 'cities and towns in plenty'. But now the Polos were heading out of the Tartar ilkhanate of Persia into a land permeated with eerie legend: Mulehet, the country of the Assassins.

The Assassins, like the Caliphs of Baghdad, were another long-recognized power which the Tartars broke in their expansion across the known world. The founder of the Assassins, Sheikh Alaodin, had been a sinister but extraordinarily gifted potentate who established for himself a power exercised by brain-washed murderers. He was known, with terrified respect, as 'The Old Man of the Mountain'. Alaodin and his successors headed the

Ismaili Moslem sect, an heretical creed of Islam founded at the end of the eleventh century. The Ismaili caliphs trained for themselves a constant supply of fanatical murderers whose only desire was to fulfil their missions and who were motivated by the certainty of attaining Paradise. This was implanted artificially. The Old Man used a special 'Paradise' constructed in a secluded valley. Into this Garden of Earthly Delights the selected trainee Assassins were carried while unconscious with drugs ('assassin' is derived from *hashashin* – 'hashish-eaters'). When they came round in the valley, they were entertained with every delightful variant of wine, women and song promised in the holy scriptures to those who would go to Paradise. Drugged again, they regained consciousness outside the valley in anguish that it had all been a dream. No, they were told, all this will be yours again on completion of your

OPPOSITE Masyaf Castle, near Hama, in Syria. This was the early twelfth-century seat of the Order of Assassins which terrified the surrounding countryside until the Tartars eliminated them.
ABOVE 'A garden like Paradise': a European artist's representation of the Old Man's Garden of Earthly Delights. From *Les Livres du Graunt Caam* (f 226).

OVERLEAF The Assassins kill Nizam al-Mulk. From the *Jami al-tavarikh*.

سيدنا عليه ما دستى كسفنة بودك قتل هذا الشيطان

دملتبة انظام الملك وحال قاصدان اوجهان سنت آملة آخرة

mission, which is to put so-and-so to death. If they survived, if they were captured, tortured or killed, the Assassins knew precisely what was waiting for them. They were men who had tasted the delights of Paradise and who had been promised that they would taste them again. Thus they were more dangerously motivated than Japan's *Kamikaze* pilots at the close of the Second World War. And as a political factor they were the supreme threat.

The list of prominent victims of the Assassins is impressive, to say the least. Two caliphs of Baghdad, a shah of Persia and a

Hulagu Khan besieges Baghdad. From a copy of the *Jami al-tavarikh* made and illustrated for the Emperor Akbar in India in 1596.

grand vizier fell to the Assassins. In addition there were the two leading Crusading lords in the Holy Land: Conrad, King of Jerusalem, and Raymond, Count of Tripoli. The two latter victims fell to the murderers sent out by the Ismaili Caliph's deputy – also known as the Old Man – who had a stronghold and Paradise of his own in the Lebanon Mountains, near Damascus.

The main Ismaili base was at Alamut, south of the Caspian, in the territory which Marco calls Mulehet. Like the last caliph of Baghdad, the last Old Man fell victim to the formidable Hulagu Khan, who finally succeeded in destroying both the castle and the Paradise after a three-year siege, in 1256.

The next stage of the march took the Polos to the cities of Shibarghan and Balkh, a route which, as Marco was very aware, was following in the footsteps of Alexander the Great, for it was in Balkh that Alexander was said to have celebrated his marriage with the daughter of Darius – that marriage which the conqueror of the world had hoped would weld East and West together. Marco described Balkh as considerably run down since the Tartars sacked it twenty-odd years before he set eyes on it. He also points out that it represented the most easterly limit of the ilkhanate. The route which the Polos were now following – Shibarghan/Balkh – was considerably to the south of the Bukhara/Samarkand route which the elder Polos had followed on their first journey to Cathay.

For the next stage of the journey Marco is unusually precise. Balkh to Talikhan: twelve days heading east-north-east. Sufficient water and game *en route*, but a deserted country, no ready food. Talikhan to Ishkasham: three days east-north-east; 'fine country all the way, thickly peopled and rich in fruits, grain, and vines'. Then a three-day journey through barren territory with the single advantage of growing enough grass for horses. This march was rewarded by reaching the province of Badakhshan, about which Marco's account becomes positively lyrical. He had good reason. It saved his life.

These mountains are so high that it takes a man a full day, from dawn to dusk, to climb from the bottom to the top. Up there are wide plateaux, with lush grass and trees and abundant springs of the purest water which plunge down over the crags to the valley below. Trout and other fine fish live in these streams. The air on the high tops is so pure and healthy that if any town valley-dweller falls ill with even the most severe kind of fever, all he has to do is to go up into the mountains and a few days' rest there will restore him to complete health. I, Messer Marco, can vouch for this from personal experience.

The choice of illnesses from which Marco could have been suffering is endless, but probably the places in which his trouble was picked up can be narrowed down to two. The first is the baking pest-hole of Hormuz, and the second could have been anywhere along the desert marches from Kerman, where the accumulated days of desert travelling on polluted or brackish water could have germinated an army of exhausting intestinal complaints. It is most unlikely, however, that 'a few days' rest' put Marco on his feet again; the Ramusio translation of the *Travels* says that he had been ill for a year, and there is a limit to the speed of convalescence from long illnesses, however beneficial the air.

A long convalescence means time to look around, and Marco certainly gave Badakhshan a detailed scrutiny. Even then, however, the mercantile streak is on the surface again: Badakhshan, he notes, was the great centre of balas ruby mining, strictly controlled by the Crown on pain of death. Second in importance to the rubies was lapis lazuli, the rich blue gem-stone, not to mention veins of silver, copper and lead in the area.

As we know from the evidence of his later experiences in China, Marco was a sportsman who loved hunting and he found this in good measure in Badakhshan: fine horses and falcons, and plenty of game.

It is likely that the anxious Niccolò and Maffeo tested the completeness of Marco's cure by taking him on a couple of short marches from Badakhshan, for at this point in the *Travels* Marco does what has not been encountered since his description of Armenia: he talks of countries off the direct line of march to Cathay. This time, however, he includes the precise number of days' journeys needed to get there. First comes Pashai, ten days to the south – a place which he clearly did not like. His tone becomes almost audibly brusque. 'The inhabitants, who have brown skins and speak a language of their own, are idolaters. They are adepts in enchantment and diabolic arts. The men wear ear-rings and brooches of gold and silver and pearls and precious stones in profusion. They are very crafty folk and artful in their own way. The climate is very hot. The stock diet is flesh and rice.' The whole curt account is the nearest Marco gets to being peevish in the *Travels*.

Seven days to the south-east of Badakhshan lay Kashmir, and here Marco displays not peevishness but inconsistency in his attitude to 'idolaters'. Neither creed nor faith is the reason for the note of tolerance which creeps into his account, but superficial custom:

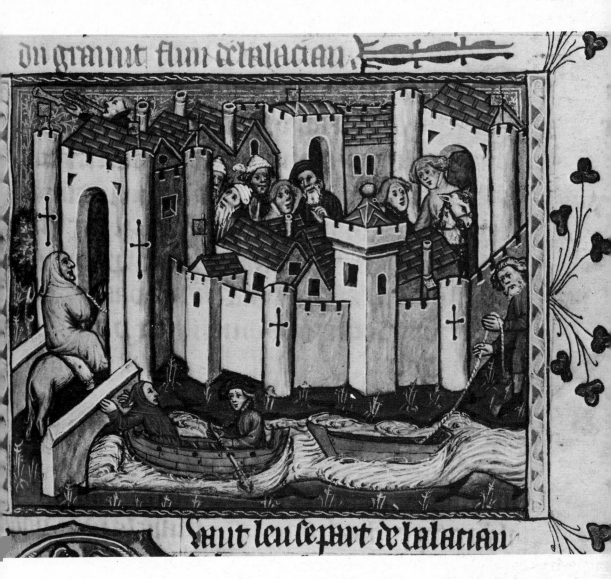

Du grannt flun de balacian

Saut leu separt de balacian

They have hermits of their own who live apart in their hermitages, fasting strictly, having nothing to do with women, and taking immense pains never to commit any sins under their law. They are considered very holy by their own folk, and they live to a great age. They live this blameless life for the love of their idols. There are also plenty of abbeys and monasteries of the same faith, where the brothers live according to a strict rule and wear tonsures like Dominican and Franciscan friars.

After this interlude, when it was apparent that Marco was fully fit again, the march was resumed, always east-north-east, always climbing. It took fifteen days to get out of Badakhshan and its

'The great river Balacian' (the upper stream of the River Oxus). This river ran through a plain of lush vegetation. From *Les Livres du Graunt Caam* (f 288).

OVERLEAF Autumn on the Pamirs in Sinkiang. Marco crossed the Pamirs in summer, when there was excellent pasturage for horses and sheep.

81

Ovis Poli, the Great Sheep of Pamir, named after Marco Polo but actually described by Guillaume de Roubrouck almost fifty years before. From *The Book of Ser Marco Polo*.

diminutive neighbour-state, Wakhan. Three more days' painful climbing took the Polos to the Roof of the World, the plain of Pamir, with the Tartars' famous river, the Oxus, flowing to the Aral Sea from Lake Sirikol. Marco did not see the place in the desolation of winter; instead he was impressed by the excellence of the pasturage – 'a lean beast grows fat here in ten days'. The most impressive animal up here was the wild sheep with great curling horns, named after Marco the *Ovis Poli*. 'From these horns the shepherds make big bowls from which they feed, and also fences to keep in their flocks. There are also innumerable wolves, which devour many of the wild rams. The horns and bones of the sheep are found in such numbers that men build cairns of them

84

beside the tracks to serve as landmarks to travellers in the snowy season.'

During their twelve-day trek across the plain of Pamir, the Polos were impressed by other phenomena. They saw no human habitation. They saw no birds. And they noticed with uneasy perplexity that fire itself had changed: it was a different colour, not so bright as elsewhere, and it did not cook well. Niccolò and Maffeo must have seen this on their first journey; to Marco it was new. He put it down to the intense cold. It was in fact caused by the altitude – the Pamir plain is 15,600 feet above sea level – which has the effect of lowering the temperature of boiling water, and thus has radical effects on the time it takes to soften rice and meat.

When the Polos had left Badakhshan, they were about as far from Peking as Niccolò and Maffeo had been when they left Bukhara in the company of the Great Khan's envoy, but further to the south. When they had reached the other side of the Pamir plain, forty days of depressing travelling lay ahead of them through the desolate country of Belor. The local inhabitants were primitive in the extreme, 'idolaters and utter savages, living entirely by the chase and dressed in the skins of beasts. They are thoroughly bad.' But after their two-month traverse of the Roof of the World, the Polos finally emerged into Kashgar province and the road sloped downward. For the elder Polos, this was familiar ground. A helpful factor, this, for having survived the ordeal of altitude and great cold, the party would now be tested by the opposite extreme: the deadly wastes of the Gobi Desert.

5 Across The Gobi

As THEY CAME DOWN from the Roof of the World, the Polos were cheered by the comparative fertility of Kashgar province. There is a note of positive relief in Marco's sketch of Kashgar: 'The inhabitants live by trade and industry. They have very fine orchards and vineyards and flourishing estates. Cotton grows here in plenty besides flax and hemp. The soil is fruitful and productive of all the means of life.' But he adds the curious note that 'the folk here are very close-fisted and live very poorly, neither eating well nor drinking well'. This indicates a touch of *naïveté* in Marco's make-up; one tends to wonder what the inhabitants of Kashgar had to put up with in the way of taxes, if their land was so kindly. 'Fine orchards and vineyards and flourishing estates' suggest a tough and rapacious feudal caste ruling in Kashgar, but Marco is silent on the point. Probably he saw none of the local lords, for it took the Polos only five days to traverse Kashgar province.

Marco was quick to add that Kashgar was 'the starting-point

PREVIOUS PAGES A desert landscape – the dreaded Gobi. Here a herd comes to drink and escape flies at the Orkhon River in south-western Mongolia, after a rare rainfall.

RIGHT Hardy Mongolian two-humped camels, used by the Mongols both for their milk and as transport. They feed on the sparse semi-desert vegetation.

from which many merchants set out to market their wares all over the world', which must have made him think of Venice and home. He goes straight on to speak of Samarkand, the great international mart and crossroads of mercantile life now lying nearly five hundred miles behind the party, away to the north-west. Niccolò and Maffeo knew Samarkand well from their previous journey, and probably held the place in that affectionate nostalgia generated by the memories of fat profits. Marco's digression on Samarkand, however, deals with another miracle testifying to the Christian faith. After pointing out that Samarkand province lay under the jurisdiction of the Great Khan's fractious nephew Kaidu, Marco tells of the days when Kubilai's brother Chagatai was alive and embraced the Christian faith. Under Chagatai's patronage a cathedral named after St John the Baptist was built in Samarkand, the local Christians rubbing in their moral victory over Islam by using a beautiful stone, held in high regard by the Moslems, to

support the central column of the building. (This was only about fifty years before King Edward I of England caused similar offence to the temporarily subjugated Scots by making off with the Stone of Scone.) After Chagatai's death the local Moslems, who out-numbered the Christians of Samarkand by ten to one, staged a comeback and prepared to remove their stone by force despite the fact that it was holding the church up. Kaidu Khan wanted no trouble and ordered the Christians to hand it over within two days. But when the stone was chiselled out, 'the column that rested on the stone rose up to a height of fully three palms and stayed there as firmly supported as if the stone had still been underneath. And from that day onwards the column has remained in this position.' It is amusing to think of the nameless architect and master mason who must have chafed a little to see the soundness of their work discounted by the wonder at this 'miracle'; the Samarkand church with its stalactite-pillar must have been one of the architectural oddities of the age, and an obvious focus for miraculous legend to the benefit of the Christian faith.

After coping with Samarkand, Marco gives a thumbnail sketch of the neighbouring province, Yarkand, also under Kaidu Khan's jurisdiction. Yarkand, like Samarkand, had a Moslem/Nestorian Christian population, and cotton was a staple crop; but Marco deemed it scarcely worthy of mention: 'there is nothing here worth mentioning in our book'. As the Polos moved out of Kashgar province, only four more staging-points separated them from the arid threshold of the last great obstacle on the road to Cathay, the Gobi Desert.

These four cities were the capitals of the most easterly provinces of Turkestan, Khotan, Pem, Charchan, and Lop. Marco's keen eye picked out the most notable peculiarities of each. At Khotan, for example, the locals were extremely prone to goitre, which Marco blames (with surprising accuracy) on the local drinking water. In the rivers of Pem province were found 'stones called jasper and chalcedony in plenty' – a clear indication of the approaching near-ness to Cathay, for this is certainly a reference to jade, so popular with Chinese jewellers. At Pem, too, 'when a woman's husband leaves her to go on a journey of more than twenty days, as soon as he has left, she takes another husband, and this she is fully entitled to do by local usage. And the men, wherever they go, take wives in the same way.' Charchan was also a noted jade source. The stones, according to Marco, 'are exported for sale in Cathay and bring in a good profit; for they are plentiful and of good quality'.

It is hard to imagine the Polos failing to take the opportunity to combine business with duty. They must have had a choice consignment of jade – however small – in their baggage when they quitted Charchan.

Marco notes the peaceful nature of all four provinces – 'they are not at all warlike'. This was hardly surprising, because for decades they had been trampled by the passing of Mongol armies setting out for their expeditions of plunder and conquest in the west. This had left its mark, and Marco gives details of how the locals reacted to the approach of hostile and friendly armies. There was little difference; enemy armies made them take off *en masse* with their animals and hide in the desert; friendly armies made them hide all their beasts 'because they do not want to have them seized and eaten; for the armies never pay for what they take'. At harvest time the corn was stored 'far from any habitation, in certain caves among these wastes, for fear of the armies; and from these stores they bring what they need month by month'. Here was the reverse side to life under the Mongols, depicted with a vengeance.

Eight days to traverse Khotan province, five days for Pem, five for Charchan and then the 'last-chance' outpost halt at Lop on the very edge of the Gobi. The travellers had had the clearest indication of what was coming: 'All this province is a tract of sand.' For the first time since the stage from Hormuz to the Persian frontier, water became the dominant problem. Once again the Polos had to get used to shortening their water ration between the dwindling number of springs of sweet water, while the surrounding terrain grew more and more arid. Lop itself was the threshold of the Gobi. 'Travellers who intend to cross the desert rest in this town for a week to refresh themselves and their beasts. At the end of the week they stock up with a month's provisions for themselves and their beasts. Then they leave the town and enter the desert.'

Marco's account of the Gobi has earned a place in any compendium of desert literature. It is not a chronicle of human endurance, nor, as in the case of Lawrence's *Seven Pillars of Wisdom*, is it replete with descriptions of the wild beauties of the desert. It is given the briefest of prefaces: 'This desert is reported to be so long that it would take a year to go from end to end; and at the narrowest point it takes a month to cross it. It consists entirely of mountains and sand and valleys. There is nothing at all to eat.' But the feeling of awe for the vastness of the desert and its effects on those hardy enough to penetrate it, is almost tangible.

91

The Mongols Today

Life has changed little for the Mongols in the past centuries. They are still a nomadic people, herdsmen and accomplished horsemen.

RIGHT A camel caravan in north China.
BELOW This Mongol can cover sixty to eighty miles a day on his pony. The fierce winds of Mongolia make it necessary for him to wear warm clothing.

ABOVE Modern Mongols
on horseback.
LEFT Mongolian horsemen
preparing for a hurdle-race.

Without Marco's story it is difficult to imagine a thirteenth-century European, brought up to respect all the superstitions of the age, coming to grips with the mirages and hallucinations exuded by the Gobi. He gives it a section all to itself. The dominant theme is the danger, which would have been dinned into the ears of the party while it was preparing for the crossing at Lop, of leaving the beaten track, and the many weird and ghostly influences which induced travellers to do so. Perhaps Messer Rustichello, to whom Marco dictated the first draft of the *Travels*, took it upon himself to inject more drama into the passage by polishing up the phraseology. But what we have is a most vivid picture of heat-haze and mirage fooling tired eyes, and the weird sounds produced by the rustle of the night wind over shifting sand:

When a man is riding through this desert by night and for some reason – falling asleep, or anything else – he gets separated from his companions and wants to rejoin them, he hears spirit voices talking to him as if they were his companions, sometimes even calling him by name. Often these voices lure him away from the path and he never finds it again, and many travellers have got lost and died because of this. Sometimes in the night travellers hear a noise like the clatter of a great company of riders away from the road; if they believe that these are some of their own company and head for the noise, they find themselves in deep trouble when daylight comes and they realise their mistake. Some men crossing this desert have seen a host of men coming towards them, suspected that they were robbers, and taken to their heels, losing the beaten track and going hopelessly astray in trying to find it again. Even during the day you can hear these spirit voices, and often you seem to hear music from many instruments – especially drums – and the clash of weapons. Because of all this, groups of travellers make a point of sticking close together. Before they go to sleep they put up a sign pointing in the direction in which they want to travel. And they hang little bells round the necks of all their animals, so that by listening to the sound they can stop them from straying off the road.

Despite these and other dangers encountered during the Gobi crossing, Marco's account suggests that the route was well established and, if adhered to, resulted in a journey of around thirty days. The first major city encountered on emerging from the wastes of the Gobi was Suchow, in Tangut province. In this region the Polos obviously stayed for some time; Marco says a year, but this is hard to imagine as the Polos were now within easy range of communication with Kubilai himself, thanks to the post-routes of western Cathay. The stay in Tangut, plus the journeys through the region which Marco subsequently made in the Great Khan's service, left its mark on the *Travels*. Marco had time to notice the social and religious customs of the province in considerable detail. In the immediate vicinity of Suchow there were the religious observances surrounding sacrifices, and the elaborate details of funerals. In Kamul province to the north-west, Marco was amazed at the Eskimo-like liberality with which the menfolk of the region treated their wives. 'If a stranger comes to a house here to seek hospitality he receives a very warm welcome. The host bids his wife do everything that the guest wishes. Then he leaves the house and goes about his own business and stays away two or three days . . . all the men of this city and province are thus cuckolded by their wives; but they are not the least ashamed of it.' Nor was this due to any plainness on the part of the womenfolk; Marco stresses that they were beautiful and 'always ready to oblige', as he puts it.

Pursuing the theme, Marco tells a story which throws an interesting sidelight on the Tartar attitude to morality. One does not normally include prudery among the virtues of the 'Mongol hordes', but the free and easy habits of Kamul province had proved too much for Mangu Khan to take and he issued a strict edict that these practices must stop. This greatly distressed the people of Kamul and they sent a deputation to the Great Khan with a rich gift and a petition that they might be allowed to keep the traditions of their ancestors. Clearly, Mangu knew when he was beaten. 'Since you desire your own shame,' he told the deputation, 'you may have it.' And so the *droit de la maison* of Kamul province survived for Marco to see for himself.

Other Tartar provinces on the fringe of the Gobi included Uighuristan, with its capital Kara Khoja, where there was a considerable population of Nestorian Christians; and Ghinghintalas, the centre of the asbestos industry. Asbestos was one of the biggest wonders to Western eyes and Marco took pains to get the true facts about 'salamander' on paper. It was derived from rich veins in the north of Ghinghintalas and was manufactured under the strict supervision of special governors appointed by the Great Khan himself.

When the stuff found in this vein has been dug out of the mountain it is pounded small, when its particles cohere and form woolly fibres. After extraction it is first dried, then pounded in a large copper mortar,

95

and washed. The residue consists of the woolly fibres and worthless earth, which is then separated out. The fibre is then carefully spun and woven into cloth.

Marco adds that the way to clean asbestos cloth was to throw it into a fire, and that a specimen was brought back from Cathay by the Polos and presented to the Pope.

From Suchow the Polos moved on to Kanchow, where they passed another long stay. From his stay here Marco chiefly remembered the social and religious habits of the local 'idolaters'. 'They avoid lechery, but do not regard it as a major sin. Their principle of conduct is that, if a woman makes love to them, they may accept her overtures without sin; but, if they make the first advances, they account that a sin.' He also notes similarities with Western practices observed by the pagan 'monks': observance of the lunar cycle and abstention from flesh-meat.

Although the Polos were now technically in Cathay – at the westernmost extremity of the Great Wall – Marco was clearly aware that they were skirting the southern fringe of the original Tartar homeland around Karakorum; and at this point in the *Travels* he embarks on a lengthy slab of Tartar history. They were in fact almost dead south of Karakorum itself at Kanchow, and only around five hundred miles away. Marco traces the route to the old Tartar capital: twelve days from Kanchow to Etinza, and then a forty-day trek across the steppe of Mongolia to Karakorum itself, which he describes as 'a city three miles in circumference, surrounded by a strong rampart of earth, because stones are scarce here'. Marco then embarks on a brief history of the rise to world supremacy of the Tartar people.

Regrettably but inevitably, this is a bewildering muddle as it stands and the confusion must be blamed on preconceived European beliefs about the Far East in Marco's time. Marco was certainly not a historian, and his version was worked up into a speculative, scholarly essay by his 'ghost-writer', Messer Rustichello of Pisa.

Western scholars had always been fascinated by the legends surrounding Prester John, the great Christian emperor 'out there' somewhere in the East, and all European travellers who journeyed East tended to look for concrete evidence of Prester John's existence. Their interest was naturally heightened by the discovery of Nestorian Christian settlements in the Far East. At the time of the journeys of Piano Carpini, Roubrouck and the Polos, two other

OPPOSITE The Great Wall of China: a modern view of the wall that was built between 246 and 209 BC. Marco, oddly enough, does not mention it, but he must have seen it.

factors had sharpened this traditional interest in Prester John. The first was the controversy surrounding a tremendous defeat inflicted on the Saracens out in Turkestan in 1148 – surely by Prester John, it was held. And the second was a piece of forgery which caused as much trouble as the Piltdown Skull and the Vinland Map rolled into one. This was the 'Letter of Prester John' to the Pope and the two Christian Emperors of the West, also dating from the middle of the twelfth century. Nobody knows who wrote it, but it expressed the goodwill of the splendid Christian power in the East towards the Christian West and was widely circulated. It was therefore reasonable for a thirteenth-century scholar to assume that Jenghiz Khan and his Tartars must have clashed with Prester John and conquered him in their rise to world supremacy, and this romantic battle of the giants actually occurs in Marco's account. But the misunderstanding is given another twist.

There was a prominent Nestorian Christian ruler in Turkestan, Togrul, who was known to the Chinese by the name Wang Khan. Roubrouck had heard of him, too, and he came to the conclusion that this Christian 'Wang Khan' must be Prester John. But it happened that a tribe living near the Great Wall of China bore the name of 'Ung', and when Marco heard of this, *he* came to the subsequent conclusion that 'Wang Khan' should in fact be rendered as 'Ung Khan', which would then make geographical sense when speaking of Tartar expansion out of Mongolia. And out of the resulting mess Marco and Rustichello spun the story which still stands in the *Travels*.

The Tartars, Marco begins, 'were a lordless people, but were actually tributary to a great lord who was called in their language Ung Khan, which simply means "Great Lord". This was that Prester John, of whose great empire the world speaks. The Tartars paid him a tribute of one beast in every ten.' But soon there was trouble. The Tartar population grew rapidly and Prester John began to worry about a possible threat from this direction. He therefore decided to re-settle the Tartars, to scatter them – 'divide and rule' in practice. But the Tartars were too quick for John. 'They were so distressed that they departed in a body and went into a desert place towards the north, where he could not trouble them. And they rebelled against his rule and withheld their tribute.' It all makes one think of the Boers and their 'Great Trek' out of Cape Colony in South Africa, or the breakaway of the Matabele from Shaka's Zulu Empire.

Then the Tartars found their leader. 'In the year of Christ's incarnation 1187 the Tartars chose a king to reign over them whose name in their language was Chinghiz Khan, a man of great ability and wisdom, a gifted orator and a brilliant soldier.' Around this paragon the Tartars rallied in their tens of thousands. And then, 'when Chinghiz Khan saw what a following he had, he equipped them with bows and their other customary weapons and embarked on a career of conquest. And I assure you that they conquered no less than eight provinces.' The snowball process continued to the point 'when he had amassed such a multitude of followers that

The battle of Jenghiz Khan and Prester John. From *Les Livres du Graunt Caam* (f 231v). The artist has again turned this into a battle typical of those fought in medieval Western Europe, injecting an Oriental touch by arming one side with scimitars.

99

they covered the face of the earth, he made up his mind to conquer a great part of the world'. The showdown with Prester John was at hand.

It began in the year 1200, when Chinghiz sent messengers to Prester John asking for the hand of his daughter. This produced an explosion of rage:

'Is not Chinghiz Khan ashamed to seek my daughter in marriage? Does he not know that he is my vassal and my thrall? Go back to him and tell him that I would sooner commit my daughter to the flames than give her to him as his wife. And tell him that my word to him is that I have good cause to put him to death as a traitor and recreant against his liege lord.' Then he bade the emissaries be gone forthwith from his presence and never return.

This insulting message incensed Chinghiz to an equal degree: 'His heart swelled within him to such a pitch that it came near to bursting within his breast. For I assure you that he had all the pride of lordship.' Vows of vengeance preceded the full and awesome muster of the Tartar host, and the invasion of Prester John's domains for a decisive battle. 'They entered a wide and pleasant plain called Tenduc, which belonged to Prester John, and there encamped. And I assure you that they were such a multitude that their number was beyond count. There he learned to his joy that Prester John was coming; for it was a pleasant plain and a spacious one, where a battle could be fought spaciously.' Both armies confronted each other on this convenient arena and prepared for battle.

Before the battle, however, Chinghiz decided to ask what the outcome would be from Christian and Saracen astrologers, and the result was the inclusion of the story of a piece of religious moral-pointing:

The astrologers then applied their skills to find out what would happen. The Saracens could not produce any results, but the Christians told him plainly. They showed him a wand which they split down the middle, putting one half on one side and one half on the other, with no one touching them. On one they put the name of Chinghiz Khan, on the other that of Prester John. Then they said to Chinghiz Khan: 'Sire, observe these wands. This half bears your name, and this bears the name of Prester John. When we have finished our incantation, the one whose half of the wand gains the upper hand will win the battle.' Chinghiz professed himself eager to see this, and told them to show him as soon as they could. Then the Christian astrologers took the psalter, read cer-

OPPOSITE A scene from one of Jenghiz Khan's battles, c. 1201. From the *Jami al-Tavarikh*.

100

tain psalms, and performed their incantation. And the wand that bore the name of Chinghiz Khan rose up without anyone touching it and positioned itself above the other wand. Chinghiz Khan was delighted to see this; and when it turned out that the Christians had been speaking the truth, he treated them with the highest respect and honour from then onwards as truthful men and true prophets.

Clearly, Marco was trying to identify Chinghiz, or Jenghiz, as closely as possible with his great hero Kubilai as far as religious toleration was concerned. Certainly the battle was a foregone conclusion: Prester John was killed, his army was routed and his empire fell to the conquering Tartars. The story – a detailed digression as it appears in the *Travels* – ends with the death of Jenghiz: 'While attacking a town named Ho-chau, he was wounded in the knee by an arrow, and of this wound he died. This was a great misfortune, since he was a brave and prudent ruler.'

Marco gets decidedly muddled in his description of the line of succession after Jenghiz Khan. He was clearly all eagerness to get to his hero, Kubilai, of whom he writes: 'all the emperors of the world and all the kings of Christians and Saracens combined would not possess such power or be able to accomplish so much as this same Kubilai, the Great Khan.' After describing the ceremonial of a Great Khan's funeral – anyone unfortunate enough to encounter the funeral cortège was put to death to serve their lord in the next world, Mangu Khan's corpse scoring over twenty thousand victims – Marco passes to the Tartars themselves. He tells of life on the steppe, of the felt-covered *yurts* drawn by oxen and camels, and of the household customs.

Marco's account of Tartar life is particularly interesting when compared to the tale of the many wonders of Chinese civilization which he was soon to see for himself. Kubilai Khan, though ruling with all the splendour of an Emperor of China, never forgot where he had come from: it is said that he had had seeds of steppe grass sown in the courtyard of the Imperial Palace so that he could always be reminded of his Tartar homeland. During his long stay in Cathay and his many conversations with Kubilai, Marco must have come to appreciate the Great Khan's awareness of his Tartar origins, and the detail in which the Tartars are described in the *Travels* suggests that he was moved to make a close study of their ways.

The first thing that impressed Marco about Tartar households was the way in which the women got on with the lion's share of the work – 'the men do not bother themselves about anything but

103

The Altai mountains –
burial-place of the
Great Khans.

hunting and warfare and falconry.' Of course this had always
been, and was to remain for centuries, the normal custom in
Europe, so there was nothing really extraordinary about it from
the European point of view. Next came diet: Tartars had an un-
discriminating taste for meat. Marco mentions game, 'Pharaoh's
rats' – steppe marmots – dogs and horsemeat.

Marco was particularly struck by the strength of family loyalties
among the Tartars. Touching another man's wife was taboo –
'they believe that such an act is disgracefully wrong.' And the
womenfolk were utterly loyal to their husbands. Strict harmony

106

Mongolian yak-breeders live in these yurts dotted along the landscape. Marco Polo described yurts but they are gradually going out of use now.

among the women was the keynote of a Tartar home (one detects a wistful note here), despite the practice of polygamy. A Tartar man could take as many wives as he liked — so long as he could support them properly. The man — not his bride — paid a dowry, to his new mother-in-law. The first wife enjoyed the highest status in the household. On the death of the head of the house the eldest son married his father's wives, but not his own mother. A man could also take on his brother's wives if they were widowed. Children were held in common and tended by all the wives in the household.

107

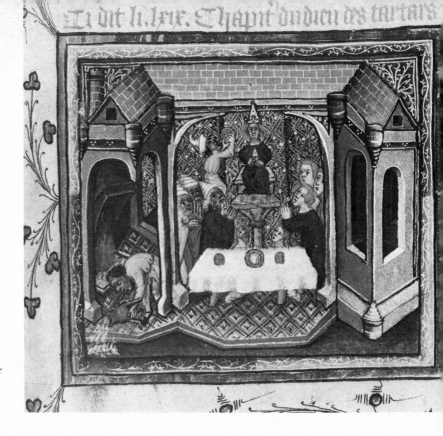

Nagatai, household god of the Tartars. On the left a Tartar pours the offering of broth on the doorstep. Inside his family pay honour to the felt puppet of Nagatai. From *Les Livres du Graunt Caam* (f 232).

Tartar religion was practical. They believed in an ethereal Supreme Being and worshipped him, 'but only for sound understanding and good health'. Of far more immediate importance was the household deity, Nagatai, the earthly god who watched over a man's children, animals and crops. Every Tartar home had its shrine with little puppets of felt and cloth depicting Nagatai, his wife and his children, all held in the deepest respect. No meal could begin without the ritual of dabbing the mouths of the images with a morsel of fat, and pouring a libation of broth on the ground outside the door as an offering to the other (un-named) spirits. And Marco rounds off his account of Tartar home life by mentioning that alcoholic standby which had impressed Roubrouck before him: 'They drink mare's milk subjected to a process that makes it like white wine and very good to drink. It is called *koumiss*.'

Despite these homely details, Marco was equally appreciative of the Tartars' mastery of the art of war and gave it equal attention. He put his finger on the most obvious reason for the Tartars' success in battle: organization and discipline, not mere weight of numbers. A Tartar army broke down into tenfold units: a troop of ten, then a hundred, a thousand, ten thousand and so on, with the result that a commander of a hundred thousand 'never needs to consult more than ten men'. Despite this tight organization, Tartar tactics in battle were the ultimate in flexibility. Feigned flight was a speciality, when the mounted bowmen could use their mobility to the full. Marco notes that Tartar warhorses were trained like sheepdogs to wheel this way or that at a touch, giving the archer the field of fire he wanted. Tartars carried out their simulated retreats while keeping up a damaging fire of arrows at the pursuing horsemen until the latter were sufficiently whittled down, and they would then launch a devastating counter-attack just when the enemy thought that he had them on the run. 'By these tactics,' comments Marco, 'they have already won many battles and conquered many nations.' But he was quick to note that much had changed in the fifty years since the death of Jenghiz. 'Nowadays their stock has degenerated. Those who live in Cathay have adopted the manners and customs of the idolaters and abandoned their own faith, while those who live in the Levant have adopted the manners of the Saracens.'

Tartar discipline was fearsome and based on flogging with rods. Offences were graded and punished with ascending numbers of

A mounted Tartar bowman in modern times. The old skills have been retained.

strokes: seven for petty offences, then seventeen, twenty-seven, thirty-seven, forty-seven and so on up to 107. The result was many deaths while undergoing such punishment. (But it was certainly no more barbaric than the British Navy's criminal code in Nelson's day, when a sentence of 'flogging round the fleet' sentenced the victim to two dozen lashes at every ship in the fleet, being revived every time he collapsed and given time to recover before the torture was resumed. Hanging was a merciful alternative.) Horse-stealing was the most common capital offence: the offender was chopped in two with a sword. But Marco states that 'if he can afford to pay, and is prepared to pay nine times the value of what he has stolen, he escapes other punishment.'

Here, clearly, at the other end of the world, is a version of the old Teutonic system of *wergild*: monetary payment in commutation of other punishment, with the amount depending on the gravity of the crime.

Concluding his account of the Tartar homeland to the north by describing the Great Khan's game reserves there, Marco turns back to the East and the last stages of the Polos' journey to Cathay. The main landmarks on the long stage through Tangut province were Erguiul, Sinju, Kalachan and Tenduc. As ever, Marco notes the main exports of each region: musk around Sinju, camel-hair cloth at Kalachan, *lapis lazuli* at Tenduc.

Then, at Chagan-nor, the party reached one of the Great Khan's regional palaces and hunting-grounds, where the most favoured prey for the royal falconer were cranes and specially-bred 'great partridges' known as *cators*. Modern gamekeepers would be fascinated to read Marco's account of how their counterparts in Kubilai's employ went about their job. Regular grain crops were sown on the hillsides for the birds alone: no one else was allowed to reap them. In winter the keepers scattered millet for the birds by hand, and the birds were so used to it that a whistle was all that was needed to summon them to feed. Special shelters were also provided for the birds, which were such a favourite with Kubilai that he had them brought to him in camel-loads during the winter months, wherever he happened to be.

By now the long journey of the Polos was nearly over and the Great Khan had been told of their approach. He sent out a royal escort to bring the travellers to his presence, 'fully forty days' journey'. Escorted with honour, the Polos came at last to the original capital of Kubilai at Shang-tu (then the summer residence) and prostrated themselves before the Great Khan.

The papal letters are presented to the Khan by the Polos. From *Les Livres du Graunt Caam* (f 220).

It was a great moment for the young Marco, and he recalled it in detail in the Prologue to the *Travels*:

They knelt before him and made obeisance with the utmost humility. The Great Khan bade them rise and received them honourably and entertained them with good cheer. He asked many questions about their condition and how they had fared after their departure. The brothers assured him that they had indeed fared well, since they found him well and flourishing. Then they presented the privileges and letters which the Pope had sent, with which he was greatly pleased, and handed over the holy oil, which he received with joy and prized very highly. When the Great Khan saw Marco, who was then a young stripling, he asked who he was. 'Sire,' said Messer Niccolò, 'he is my son and your liege man.' 'He is heartily welcome,' said the Khan. What need to make a long story of it? Great indeed were the mirth and merry-making with which the Great Khan and all his Court welcomed the arrival of these emissaries. And they were well served and attended to in all their needs. They stayed at Court and had a place of honour above the other barons.

After seven hundred years we can still sense the Polos' relief that after all the frustration, disappointment and exhaustion of their long journey, Kubilai passed so generously over the fact that their mission had not been accomplished as he had asked.

111

6 The Great Khan

THE POLOS' GRATIFICATION at their safe arrival in Cathay – not to mention their relief that Kubilai had not taken offence because their mission had not been a total success – would have been modified if they had known that they were in for a seventeen-year stay. It was during this long period that Marco became the dominant member of the trio. After all, during the journey he had been little more than a passenger, with the main decisions being taken by Niccolò and Maffeo. It is true that we have only Marco's version to go by, but certainly the Great Khan found much in the perceptive and intelligent young man that was missing in the elder Polos. Marco, in turn, reacted to Kubilai's affability with a gratitude which very soon turned to hero-worship.

The content of the *Travels*, after taking the reader safely to Cathay, makes one think of a computer struggling to do its job although jammed with excessive data. It is remarkable that Marco remembered so many details, but they do make it hard to see the wood for the trees. One theme takes over right from the start: the magnificence of Kubilai and his ability as a ruler. There at least we are on comparatively firm ground.

A description of Kubilai's summer palace was one of Marco's first concerns. It was dove-tailed into the walled city of Shang-tu, and included sixteen miles of enclosed park-land outside the city walls. Inside this royal estate Kubilai pitched his portable palace: a pre-fabricated structure made of sliced bamboo cane, held in position by silken guy-ropes. This palace was the centre of Kubilai's summer hunting; the park was stocked with deer which served the double purpose of affording sport for Kubilai and providing food for his hawks. Marco was particularly impressed by Kubilai's mew of gerfalcons, the prerogative of emperors – the Great Khan had over two hundred of them. Marco also tells of Kubilai's rides into the park with a leopard (probably a cheetah) on the crupper of his horse, which he would release to bring down a deer to feed his gerfalcons.

Two other subjects stuck in Marco's mind during the stay at Shang-tu. The first of these was the presence of 'astrologers and enchanters' from Tibet and Kashmir. These were the *Bakhshis*, the magicians whom Kubilai had hoped to see confounded by the superior aura of Christian priests from Europe. Their presence, according to Marco, ensured the Great Khan constant good weather during his visits to Shang-tu, and their most famous trick was sending Kubilai's drinking-cups floating through the air to his hand 'in the sight of ten thousand men'.

PREVIOUS PAGES The palace of the Khanate: Peking or Khanbalig, the centre of Kubilai's empire. From *Le Livre des Merveilles*.

OPPOSITE A watchtower on the walls of Peking, the Forbidden City.

115

Marco's other dominant memory of Shang-tu is the impressive propitiation-rite always carried out on the Great Khan's departure after his three-month stay (June, July and August every year). The ceremony took place on 28 August, and it centred on the imperial stud of white stallions and mares – 'the mares alone amount to more than ten thousand'. It took the form of a libation to the spirits, using the milk of the white mares, 'in order that they may guard all his possessions, men and women, beasts, birds, crops and everything besides'.

Marco's account of Kubilai himself and the life-style of the imperial family is certainly a human one, magnificent though it is.

'He is a man of good stature, neither short nor tall, but of moderate height. His limbs are well fleshed out and modelled in due proportion. His complexion is fair and ruddy like a rose, the eyes black and handsome, the nose shapely and set squarely in place' – a timely reminder that the stock Tartar image of slit eyes, high cheek-bones and yellow skin is a misleading one. Chinese stylization is stamped all over all attempts to depict Kubilai in portraiture, but even so it is possible to detect a whimsical twinkle in the eyes and a tendency to smile in the generous mouth.

Kubilai had four wives, all of them held in the highest honour. There was no 'chief wife'.

His eldest son by any of these four has a rightful claim to be emperor on the death of the present Khan. They are called empresses, each by her own name. Each of these ladies holds her own Court, and none of them has less than three hundred ladies-in-waiting, all of great beauty and charm. They are attended by many eunuchs and many other men and women, so that each one of these ladies has in her Court ten thousand persons.

Marco was fascinated by the selection of Kubilai's concubines and obviously put not a little discreet research into the method followed. Despite the fact that he was overlord of Eurasia, Kubilai favoured Kungurat province as the special recruiting-ground for his young ladies, 'a very good-looking race with fair complexions'. The recruiting was done by talent scouts appointed by Kubilai, whose first task was to gather together the likeliest candidates – 'some four or five hundred, more or less'. These were then subjected to a beauty competition, feature by feature, with marks being awarded up to twenty. After this first weeding-out, another judging by other valuers reduced the number to thirty or forty top-scorers. These were then handed over to the barons' wives,

OPPOSITE Two views of the Forbidden City as it now stands:
TOP A sun-dial within the city.
BOTTOM The walls of the palace.

116

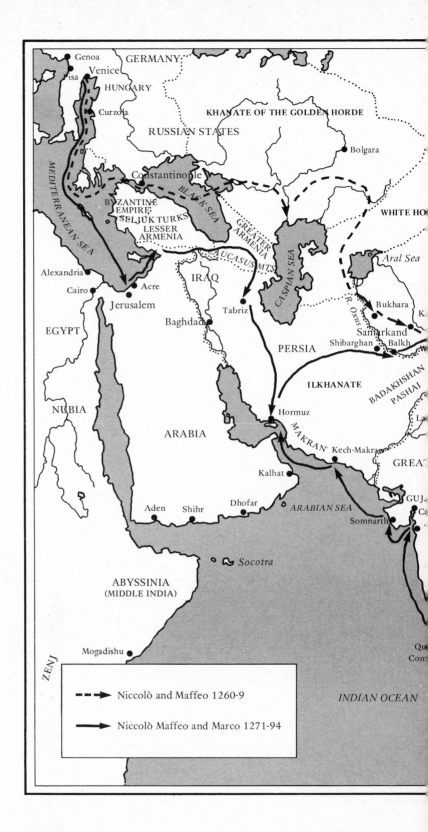

Genoa
Venice
Pisa
GERMANY
HUNGARY
Curzola
RUSSIAN STATES
KHANATE OF THE GOLDEN HORDE
Bolgara
Constantinople
BYZANTINE
EMPIRE
SELJUK TURKS
LESSER
ARMENIA
BLACK SEA
GREATER
ARMENIA
WHITE HO
Aral Sea
MEDITERRANEAN SEA
CAUCASUS MTS
CASPIAN SEA
R. Oxus
Bukhara
K
Samarkand
Alexandria
Cairo
Acre
Jerusalem
IRAQ
Tabriz
Baghdad
PERSIA
Shibarghan
Balkh
ILKHANATE
BADAKHSHAN
PASHAI
EGYPT
NUBIA
ARABIA
Hormuz
MAKRAN
Kech-Makran
GREAT
L
Kalhat
GUJ
Ca
Aden
Shihr
Dhofar
ARABIAN SEA
Somnarth
Socotra
ABYSSINIA
(MIDDLE INDIA)
Mogadishu
ZENJ
Qu
Com
INDIAN OCEAN

- - - ▶ Niccolò and Maffeo 1260-9

───▶ Niccolò Maffeo and Marco 1271-94

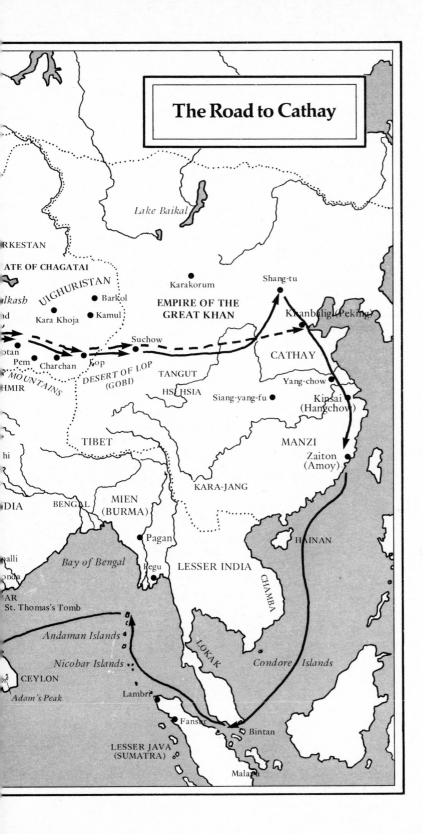

The Road to Cathay

RKESTAN

ATE OF CHAGATAI

UIGHURISTAN

Lake Baikal

Barkol

Kara Khoja   Kamul

Karakorum

Shang-tu

EMPIRE OF THE GREAT KHAN

Khanbaligh Peking

Suchow

Pem   Charchan   Lop

MOUNTAINS

DESERT OF LOP (GOBI)

TANGUT

HSI HSIA

CATHAY

Yang-chow

Siang-yang-fu

Kinsai (Hangchow)

TIBET

KARA-JANG

MANZI

Zaiton (Amoy)

DIA   BENGAL

MIEN (BURMA)

Pagan

HAINAN

Bay of Bengal   Regu

LESSER INDIA

CHAMBA

St. Thomas's Tomb

Andaman Islands

LOKAK

Condore Islands

Nicobar Islands

CEYLON

Adam's Peak   Lambri

Fansur   Bintan

LESSER JAVA (SUMATRA)

Malayu

who were briefed 'to observe them carefully at night in their chambers, to make sure that they are virgins and not blemished or defective in any member, that they sleep sweetly without snoring, and that their breath is sweet and they give out no unpleasant odour'. Having passed all these exhaustive tests, the successful candidates were divided into groups of six and served Kubilai on a rota system, a new group every three days. 'While some of the group are in attendance in their lord's chamber, the others wait in an ante-chamber close by. If he needs anything from outside, such as food or drink, the girls inside the chamber pass word to those outside, who immediately get it ready.'

Kubilai's preference for this idyllic service was by no means totally selfish. It was considered a great honour to have a daughter considered worthy for concubinage. Nor did the lower scorers suffer. On the contrary, 'They remain with the Khan's other women in the palace, where they are instructed in needlework, glove-making and other elegant accomplishments. When some nobleman is looking for a wife, the Great Khan gives him one of these girls with a great dowry. And in this way he marries them all off honourably.'

Marco then passes to Kubilai's children. The Great Khan had twenty-two sons by his four wives. The eldest, Chinkim, was the Crown Prince, although he was destined to die before Marco quitted China, leaving his own son, Temur, as heir-apparent. Kubilai's sons were all groomed for government. 'Seven are kings of great provinces and kingdoms. They all exercise their authority well, lacking neither prudence nor prowess.' The concubines gave Kubilai another twenty-five sons, 'all good men and brave soldiers. And each of them is a great baron.'

After describing Kubilai's private household, Marco turns to the capital of the Great Khan's empire, Khanbalig, and the main imperial palace. The detail in this passage is so dense that it amounts to a guided tour. After seventeen years, after all, anyone might be expected to know the place thoroughly. Marco begins with a description of the palace, raised above ground-level on a podium within two concentric walls:

The roof of the palace itself is very high. The walls of the halls and chambers inside are all covered with gold and silver and decorated with pictures of dragons and birds and horsemen and various breeds of beasts and battle-scenes. The ceiling is similarly decorated – nothing but gold and pictures everywhere. The hall is so vast and so wide that a meal might well be served there for more than six thousand men. The number

120

of chambers is quite bewildering. The whole palace is at once so immense and so well constructed that no one in the world, granted that he had the resources, could imagine any improvement in design or execution. The roof blazes with scarlet and green and blue and yellow and every colour, so brilliantly varnished that it glitters like crystal and the sparkle of it can be seen from far away. And this roof is strong and stoutly built to last for many a year.

In the rear of the palace are extensive apartments, both chambers and halls, in which are kept the private possessions of the Khan. Here is stored his treasure: gold and silver, precious stones and pearls, and his gold and silver vessels. And here too are his ladies and his concubines. In these apartments everything is arranged for his comfort and convenience, and outsiders are not admitted.

A similar palace had been built for Prince Chinkim. Their parks clearly show Kubilai's talents as a landscape designer, for he had made good use of the soil excavated from the vast stew-ponds in the palace grounds. It had been heaped into a natural hill and planted with superb trees, all evergreens. Kubilai selected them himself and was wont to make additions whenever he heard of a particularly fine specimen, no matter from how far away. As a final touch he had had the mound covered with green *lapis lazuli*, and a green palace built on top. 'I give you my word', concludes Marco, 'that mound and trees and palace form a vision of such beauty that it gladdens the hearts of all beholders. It was for the sake of this entrancing view that the Great Khan had them constructed, as well as for the refreshment and recreation they might afford him.'

In describing Kubilai's capital, Marco was nevertheless forced to make the point that it was the capital of an alien race. The Great Khan had heard that Khanbalig was destined by prophecy to be the seat of rebellion. He had reacted by building a completely new city, Taidu, across the river from old Khanbalig, and transferring the reliable city population there. (How the reliable elements were selected, Marco does not say.) Kubilai's new capital had an overall 'circumference' of twenty-four miles and was built in the form of a square. There were twelve massive gates, each guarded by a thousand men. The strictest order was maintained inside the walls. Even funeral cremations took place outside the suburbs. In the suburbs, too, was the 'red light' district, with the almost unbelievable population of twenty thousand prostitutes. They were organized with frightening efficiency, headed by a captain-general, with chiefs-of-thousand and chiefs-of-hundred respon-

LEFT An aerial view across
the mountains of
Afghanistan, the 'Roof of
the World'.
ABOVE The entrance to the
palace district of the Khans
in Ulan Bator.

sible to her. Details are too much for Marco when he turns to the wealth of the city; it is the centre for everything, and he tries to convey the magnitude of the city's revenue by pointing out that *every day* over a thousand cart-loads of silk entered Khanbalig.

Superlatives fail even Marco when it comes to describing Court protocol and the splendour of Kubilai's banquets. It is hard to imagine a state dinner where *over forty thousand* of the guests dine outside the main hall. Following Tartar superstition, two huge guardians prevented any man from touching the threshold of the hall on pain of fines or physical beating. (Strangers had barons assigned to them to warn them of the custom.) Whenever Kubilai raised his cup to drink, music sounded and the entire company knelt in humility. The lords who waited on the Great Khan himself had their mouths and noses 'swathed in fine napkins of silk and gold, so that the food and drink are not contaminated by their breath or effluence'.

Kubilai's birthday (28 September) saw the greatest feast of the year, when he wore solid gold robes and twelve thousand of his barons and knights wore cloth-of-gold and silk in imitation. Next came the White Feast – the Tartar New Year, celebrated in February. Every one of the lunar months of the year had a feast of its own, in which the twelve thousand would wear robes of the same colour: thirteen sets in all.

Sportsman that he was, Marco was equally staggered by the extent of Kubilai's hunting establishment. The Great Khan hunted generally in winter months in Khanbalig (December, January and February). He had two 'masters of hounds', the brothers Bayan and Mingan, each of whom had ten thousand subordinates. One group wore red livery, the other blue; and when the Great Khan rode out to hunt, one ten thousand went on one side, one on the other. As each group had five thousand hounds, it must have been an impressive sight. Falconry, however, was Kubilai's passion. Marco describes his travelling hunting-lodge with its gold lining, carried by four elephants, where Kubilai always kept twelve gerfalcons. There was a trap-door in the roof through which Kubilai could launch his gerfalcons without leaving his couch.

Because of his own enthusiasm for the subject, Marco was human enough in giving far more detailed attention to the excellence of Kubilai's hunting than to the more boring realities of how the Mongol Empire was governed; but he does not neglect the latter in the *Travels*. Although it is a comparatively short passage, it shows that Marco grasped the obvious fact that the fundamental

power behind the Tartar supremacy was military, and that both military and civilian structures of government were needed to keep the wheels turning in Kubilai's empire. Although the military machine came first, both clearly relied upon considerable delegation of powers.

Twelve lords appointed by Kubilai saw to the armies. They were the men who decided what troops should be moved where, who should be appointed to high commands, and what forces were needed for whatever crisis arose. They were also responsible for supervising the appointment and promotion of the best commanders – a constant sifting process which also served to weed out officers who had proved themselves cowardly or incompetent.

Mongol horsemen hunting with hawks at the turn of the century.

125

Mongol horsemen lassoing animals (horses or wolves) at a great distance using twenty-foot catching poles with lasso rope fastened at the end. The wind is too strong for them to use rope only.

The result was a constant series of promotions and demotions. A captain of a hundred who did well in an engagement would be rewarded by promotion to captain of a thousand; a captain of ten thousand who bungled a campaign would be demoted to the command of a thousand, and so on. Kubilai, however, kept his finger on the pulse: all such military rewards or punishments were submitted to the Great Khan for his *fiat*. The military council-of-twelve, called the *Thai*, was only responsible to Kubilai himself.

One of Kubilai Khan's bowmen – after a Chinese drawing of the period.

The civil authority was organized on similar lines. The thirty-four provinces which made up Kubilai's domains were governed by a council of twelve barons also appointed by the Great Khan. This civilian cabinet had its seat in a special palace at Khanbalig: a self-contained civil service with its own offices and staff. Every province was regulated by a judge with a staff of his own, with permanent quarters in the palace. Under the council of twelve, the provincial governors handled the day-to-day business of running

127

Medieval Tartar huts (yurts) and wagons, with a mounted bowman in the right-hand corner. From *The Book of Ser Marco Polo*.
OPPOSITE A typical feudal scene in Mongolia: an old bell-tower, the bells still intact, and in the foreground the nomads' yurts.

the provinces. Their appointment, as with the promotions and demotions in the army, was decided by the council and ratified by Kubilai. The duties of the governors embraced every facet of civilian life and included tax-collecting and public expenditure, but stopped short of any overlap with the affairs of the army. This council was named the *Shieng*.

'Both the *Thai* and the *Shieng*', Marco concludes, 'are supreme courts, having no authority above them except the Great Khan himself, and enjoying the power to confer great benefits on whom they will. The *Thai*, however, that is to say the military court, is esteemed more highly and carries greater dignity than any other office.'

Despite the emphasis and significance of the last sentence, the overall picture of a powerful, centralized government divided into military and civilian spheres is an impressive one. From Marco's own observations, let alone from those conveyed in the Chinese records for the period, it is obvious that it was a successful and beneficent machine. The machine ran itself, but Kubilai was chief engineer. What gives him a special place high up on the list of the despots of world history is that he relied absolutely on the delegation of authority, which could go wrong only in one way: by the

128

selection of the wrong man for the job. And he himself had the final responsibility in putting such mistakes to rights.

In sharp contrast to the splendour of the imperial Court, Marco was struck by the extent and efficiency of public assistance. Families hit by bad luck or illness could register for a year's subsidy, which could be paid the following year on production of the receipt for the previous year's payment. This assistance included clothing, for every craft had to deliver the production of one day in every week as a tithe to the Great Khan. These fabrics were specially stored and issued to the poor as winter and summer clothing. Marco added that this munificence was something that the Tartars had learned from their new subjects, the Chinese:

You must understand that according to their ancient customs, before they became familiar with the doctrines of the idolaters, the Tartars never used to give alms. Indeed, when a poor man came to them, they would drive him off with curses, saying: 'Go with God's curse upon you! If he had loved you as he loves me, he would have blessed you with prosperity!' But since the sages of the idolaters, in particular the *Bakhshi* of whom I have spoken above, persuaded the Great Khan that it was a good work to provide for the poor and that their idols would be greatly pleased by it, he decided to make such provision as I have described. No one who goes to his Court in quest of bread is ever turned away empty-handed. Everyone receives a portion. And not a day passes but twenty or thirty thousand bowls of rice, millet and panic are doled out and given away by the officials. . . .

Apart from the immense scale, Marco was on firm ground when describing Kubilai's ceremonial, hunting and public assistance: they were all to be found on a smaller scale in Europe. But there were some phenomena which were totally new to him. The first we have already met, asbestos, but the other three beggared his imagination, and they were paper currency, coal and the imperial post.

There had been a few scattered and generally unknown experiments with token currency in Europe but the basic idea was a total surprise even to the mercantile Polos. Gold and silver were gold and silver, and purchased goods in straight exchange for value. How could paper substitute? 'You might well say that he [the Great Khan] has mastered the art of alchemy,' is Marco's amazed comment, and he attributes the success of paper money to Kubilai's stature as a ruler. 'With these pieces of paper they can buy anything and pay for anything. And I can tell you that the papers that reckon as ten bezants do not weigh one.'

130

Marco never grasped the idea that paper notes were an expression of credit – of the Khan's written promise to pay the amount described – even though he recorded that each note bore the signatures and stamps of treasury officials. All he saw was that the practice enabled Kubilai to impound all bullion and gems in his dominions and issue paper in exchange, so that 'all the world's great potentates put together do not have such riches as belong to the Great Khan alone'. Even Kubilai was not powerful enough to stave off inflation. He did in fact end up by printing more notes than he had bullion in his vaults, and found it necessary to issue new notes in 1287 (five years before the Polos left China for home), by which time devaluation had made one of the new notes worth five of the old.

Marco's expressions of wonder at 'stones that burn like logs' show us how ignorant even a man of a leading Mediterranean sea-

The Khan distributes alms. Not only did Kubilai give aid to the poor; he also subsidized provinces in times of scarcity caused by bad weather. From *Les Livres du Graunt Caam* (f 244v).

131

power could be in the thirteenth century. Coal was by no means unknown in Europe: fumes from crude, 'sea-coal' fires had been causing a smog problem in London for decades. But coal was new to Marco. 'These stones keep a fire going better than wood . . . if you put them on the fire in the evening and see that they are well alight, they will continue to burn all night, so that you will find them still glowing in the morning.' Marco found coal throughout China.

It is true that they have plenty of firewood, too. But the population is so enormous and there are so many bath-houses and baths constantly being heated, that it would be impossible to supply enough firewood, since there is no one who does not visit a bath-house at least three times a week and take a bath – in winter every day, if he can manage it. Every man of rank or means has his own bathroom in his house . . . so these stones, being very plentiful and very cheap, effect a great saving of wood.

Marco's reference to baths raises another point: the Oriental obsession with bodily cleanliness. After their seventeen-year stay in China, Marco, Niccolò and Maffeo were probably the cleanest Europeans known for centuries!

The Khan hunts deer. From *Les Livres du Graunt Caam* (f 240v).

Although Marco's surprise at coal would not have been shared

throughout the Europe of his day, the imperial post was totally different and nothing like it had been seen in the world since the Roman Empire. There were three main grades of despatch, which may be rendered in modern terms as 'second class', 'first class' and 'On His Imperial Majesty's Service: Top Priority'.

'Second class' messages were carried by foot-runners, who had relay-stations three miles apart. Each messenger wore a special belt hung with small bells to announce his approach and ensure that his relief was out on the road and ready for a smooth take-over. This system enabled a message to cover the distance of a normal ten-day journey in twenty-four hours. At each three-mile station a log was kept on the flow of messages and all the routes were patrolled by inspectors. 'First-class' business was conveyed on horseback, with relay-stages of twenty-five miles. But the really important business of Kubilai's empire was carried by non-stop despatch-riders carrying the special tablet with the sign of the gerfalcon. At the approach to each post-house the messenger would sound his horn; the ostlers would bring out a ready-saddled fresh horse, the messenger would transfer to it and gallop straight off. Marco affirms that this gruelling technique enabled messages to be flashed 250 or 300 miles in a day, although he admits that this required horsemen of exceptional stamina who were 'very highly prized'.

Marco was greatly impressed with the Cathayan upper classes with whom he came into contact at the Court of Kubilai and, later, while about his official business in the Khan's service. He has nothing but praise for their manners, but reflects all the layman's lack of comprehension at their intellectual gifts and religious beliefs. Buddhism, as we shall see, came to interest him considerably, but he never really grasped the significance of the Buddhist theory of the transmigration of the soul, which he records just like any other of the myriad weird practices he encountered on his travels. Behind the words of the following passage we can see Marco as an honest outsider recording the superficial symptoms of a culture and mentality which is completely incomprehensible to him:

No other nation can match them for the excellence of their manners and their knowledge of many subjects, since they devote much time to study and to the acquisition of knowledge. Their speech is pleasant and restrained; they greet one another courteously and cheerfully; they are dignified in their demeanour, cleanly at table and so forth. But they have no regard for the welfare of their souls, caring only for the nurture

133

LEFT The Great Khan with
three of his wives and some
of his sons. In fact he had
four wives, and twenty-two
legitimate sons, according to
Marco Polo's account. From
Le Livre des Merveilles.
ABOVE The Khan's birthday
party, one of the outstanding
occasions in the year.
From *Les Livres du Graunt
Caam* (f 239).

Kubilai Khan crossing a
bridge of boats during his
campaign to conquer
southern China.
(Asiatic Society of Bengal
MS D.31, f 105).

of their bodies and for their own happiness. Concerning the soul, they certainly believe that it is immortal, but in the following way. They hold that as soon as a man dies his soul enters into another body; and depending on how well or how badly he has behaved in life, he passes from good to better or from bad to worse. That is to say, if he is a man of humble rank and has behaved well and virtuously in life, he will be reborn after death from a gentlewoman and will be a gentleman, and after that, reborn yet again from a noblewoman, he will become a nobleman; and so he follows an ever-upward path culminating into assumption into the Deity. But if he is a man of good birth and has behaved badly, he will be reborn as the son of a peasant; from a peasant's life he will pass to a dog's, and so continually downwards.

This interpretation of the Noble Eight-Fold Path of Salvation as a sort of spiritual Debrett is touching. We can imagine the learned Buddhists of Cathay patiently trying to leave Marco, this influential foreigner with the untrained and crude mind, with the correct opinion of their message. But even if they had been dealing not with Marco but with the best brains of thirteenth-century Europe, the result would have been much the same. It would have been like trying to instruct Roger Bacon in the basics of nuclear physics before he had mastered the art of making gunpowder.

As far as codes of conduct in this world were concerned, Marco singled out three particular instances for special mention in the following sequence:

They treat their father and mother with profound respect. If it should happen that a child does anything to displease his parents or fails to remember them in their need, there is a department of state with the sole function of imposing severe penalties on those found guilty of such ingratitude.

Those criminals who are caught and put in prison, if not set free at the time appointed by the Great Khan for the release of prisoners (which recurs every three years), are then set free; but they are branded on the jaw, so that they may be recognized.

The present Khan prohibited all the gambling and cheating that used to be more prevalent among them than anywhere else in the world. To cure them of the habit he would say: 'I have acquired you by force of arms and all that you possess is mine. So, if you gamble, you are gambling with my property.' He did not, however, make this an excuse to extort anything from them.

Here again we have Marco bearing witness to the delicate synthesis which made up the power of Kubilai Khan: the act of military conquest which had created it, and the sensitivity and fairness – and, one might almost add in the case of the prohibited gambling, the humour – with which it was maintained.

Such, in brief, was the extraordinary monarch whose service Marco was about to join, which would familiarize the young Venetian with the furthest extent of Mongol China and enable him to speak of Kubilai Khan and his empire with all the authority of a Crown official.

7 Lord of Cathay

MARCO SEEMS TO HAVE impressed Kubilai from the beginning. It is hardly surprising. His memory for places and customs, and his flair for picking up dialects (aided to a considerable extent by the experience of his father and uncle), must have stood out as soon as Kubilai asked the young man how he had found the journey. The briefest examination of the scope of the *Travels* makes one think of William the Conqueror's 'Doomsday Book', that classic of medieval record-compiling that reads like a computer print-out. Here were talents that any ruler would find invaluable, and Marco was quite aware of the fact. He made sure that Kubilai knew it, too, and his own account in the Prologue of the *Travels*, though not exactly remarkable for its modesty, is worth quoting in full:

It happened that Marco, Messer Niccolò's son, acquired an impressive knowledge of the customs of the Tartars, their dialects and their letters. It is a fact that before he had been very long at the Great Khan's Court he had mastered four languages with their methods of writing. He was unusually wise and intelligent and the Great Khan was very well disposed to him because of the exceptional qualities that he saw in him. Noting his intelligence, the Khan sent him on an official visit to a country named Kara-jang, which it took him a good six months to reach. The young man fulfilled his mission excellently. He had noticed for himself more than once that when the messengers sent out by the Khan to various parts of the world returned to him and gave an account of their missions, they had very little else to say. Their master would then call them dolts and blockheads, saying that he would rather hear reports on these strange countries and their customs and usages than the official business on which he had sent them. When Marco went on his mission he was well aware of this, and he paid close attention to all the novelties and curiosities that came his way, so that he could describe them to the Great Khan. When he returned he presented himself to the Khan and started with a full account of the business on which he had been sent – he had accomplished it well. Then he went on to describe all the remarkable things he had seen on the journey, in such detail that the Khan and all those who heard him were amazed and said to each other: 'If this young man lives to reach full manhood, he will certainly prove himself a man of sound judgment and worth.' Need I go on? From then on the young man was called Messer Marco Polo; and so he will be called throughout this book. And with good reason, for he was a man of experience and discretion.

All in all, this version tends to give the rather unpleasant impression of an ambitious young man on the make; but one point worth bearing in mind is that Kubilai was an alien overlord over many countries, not a native-born Chinese emperor. Foreigners were naturally encouraged under his regime; they had their own district quarters in Khanbalig; they had equal chances of serving the Great Khan. And Marco's own career in Kubilai's service was considerably accelerated by the fact that he was on the spot during an extremely dangerous *coup d'état* staged by the Chinese in about 1277.

The plot was germinated by the general hatred engendered by Kubilai's *Bailo* or lord-lieutenant, a Moslem named Ahmad who enjoyed the complete faith of the Great Khan and literally got away with murder. According to Marco, 'whenever he wished to cause the death of anyone whom he hated, whether justly or unjustly, he would go to the Emperor and say to him: "So-and-so deserves to die, because he has offended your Majesty in such-and-such a way." Then the Emperor would say: "Do as you think best." And Ahmad would thereupon put him to death.' Ahmad rapidly became adept at every form of financial and political corruption and became the most hated man in Cathay. Two Chinese officers in Kubilai's service, Wan-hu and Ch'ien-hu, planned the assassination of Ahmad as the prelude to a national rising in which every 'foreign devil' would perish, and China be freed. 'Kill the bearded men,' was the watchword. When all was ready, Ahmad was summoned to the palace by a fake message from Prince Chinkim, while both Kubilai and Chinkim were enjoying their annual stay at Shang-tu.

What happened next reads so vividly in the *Travels* that Marco must have been an eye-witness. Wan-hu was seated on the throne, with a blaze of lights before him to assist the deception. When Ahmad was summoned, he was extremely surprised and suspicious, but he went.

As he went in through the city gates he met a Tartar officer named Kogatai, commander of the twelve thousand who kept constant watch over the city. 'Where are you going to at such a late hour?' asked Kogatai. 'To Chinkim, who has just arrived.' 'How can he have arrived so secretly that I have heard nothing about it?' asked Kogatai, and he followed with a detachment of the guard. . . . The moment Ahmad entered the palace and saw such a blaze of lights, he knelt before Wan-hu, thinking he was Chinkim; and Ch'ien-hu, who was there armed with a sword, cut off his head. . . .

When Kogatai, who had halted at the entrance to the palace, saw what had happened he shouted 'Treason!' and immediately shot an arrow at Wan-hu, who was seated on the throne, killing him. Then, calling on his men, he seized Ch'ien-hu. And he issued a proclamation throughout the city that anyone found out of doors would be killed on the spot.

143

The Chü-yang Gate, in Hopeh Province. It is the closest gate in the Great Wall to Peking.

The rising was nipped in the bud; the call to arms never reached the other cities of China. Kubilai, informed by courier, gave Kogatai full powers to conduct an investigation until his own return. When the Great Khan finally returned to Khanbalig, there was a full enquiry at which Marco gave evidence. Kubilai's reaction was savage: Ahmad's corpse was flung into the street to be shredded by dogs, those of his sons who were found guilty of similar crimes in their father's heyday were flayed alive and severe restrictive laws cracked down on the former freedom of the Moslem population. Kubilai's opinion of Marco as a frank and honest reporter was undoubtedly enhanced by this affair, and Marco's career as a 'travelling privy councillor' seems to have begun soon after. After the shock caused by such dangerous events in his own capital, Kubilai would certainly have wanted accurate reports on what was going on in the provinces.

It is significant that the destination of Marco's first journey in the Khan's service was the province where Tartar armies were still fighting a 'brush-fire' war: Kara-jang, adjacent to Burma, far away to the south-west. Just how long it took him we do not know, for he contradicts himself: in the Prologue he says six months (from Khanbalig), in the main narrative of the *Travels* he says four. But it certainly took him across the breadth of Old Cathay – between the Great Wall and the Yangtse-kiang river. And an illustration of the contrasts he saw might be drawn by a trip from the peaceful southern states of India under the British Raj across the Khyber Pass into Afghanistan, from where all was law and order to the frontier that was never at rest.

Marco was not ten miles out of Khanbalig before he was marvelling at the massive ornamental bridge across the Hun-ho river: twenty-four arches, nearly three hundred yards long, and able to take ten horsemen riding abreast. For once Marco was probably right when he asserted that there was no other bridge in the world like it. Thirty miles on lay Cho-chow, another ten-day journey to T'ai-yuan-fu, a wine and silk centre, then seven more days to P'ing-yang-fu. Nearby lay the ancient castle of Caichu, said to have been built by a legendary character called the 'Golden King'. The story went that he had challenged the power of Prester John in the days before the Tartars came, but had been kidnapped by John and set to work herding cows for two years. After this period John had asked his captive if he still thought himself able to make war against his lord. The Golden King admitted he was not, whereupon John released him and let him go home – a lesson to all loyal

146

vassals. This is precisely the sort of local legend which Kubilai would have relished and it is safe to imagine Marco telling it to the Khan. Apart from its nice moral twist, it would have been politically welcome to Kubilai after the attempted Chinese *putsch*.

Twenty more miles brought Marco to the Kara-moran river – the Hwang-ho. Across the Kara-moran lay the city of Ho-chung-fu, and eight days further on to the south-west Si-ngan-fu, a provincial capital under the rule of Mangalai Khan, one of Kubilai's sons. Marco gave Mangalai a good report as a ruler, albeit a somewhat hackneyed one: just, upright and loved by his subjects. The hunting on his estates was good, too.

Continuing on this south-westerly heading for another twenty-three days, Marco traversed Han-chung and Ak-balik Manzi provinces and reached the city of Ch'êng-tu-fu (modern Chungking) on the Kiang-sui (Yangtse) river. This city was another provincial capital – but only another five days' travelling was needed to reach

The bridge of Pulisanghin, from a Chinese original. From *The Book of Ser Marco Polo.*

OVERLEAF The Hsi-ling Gorge on the Yangtse-kiang. It is famous for its rapids and powerful currents.

147

The Garden-House on the Lake at Yunnan-fu. This lake was described by Marco Polo as being nearly a hundred miles round its circumference.

the wild terrain on the outer confines of Cathay. Marco calls this frontier province 'Tibet', but it was clearly far to the east of the modern country of that name. The present Chinese provinces of Szechwan and Yunnan seem to be nearer the mark.

Marco's first impression of 'Tibet' was one of ruins and destruction: the place had been ravaged by Mangu Khan and had never recovered. Here again was a fresh, outsider's verdict which no ordinary Tartar envoy would probably have brought to Kubilai's notice. In 'this desolate country, infested by dangerous wild beasts', Marco was particularly impressed by the forests of giant bamboo and by the terrifying drumfire of explosions which broke out when they caught fire. He also adds the only way for travellers to stop their horses from bolting in panic at the sound. Halters and heel-ropes are not enough: the proper way is to bandage the horses' eyes and hobble their feet with iron fetters. 'Then, when they hear the crackling of the canes, however hard they try to bolt, they cannot do it.' But Tibet was not totally depressing for travellers: Marco noted that local custom regarded virginity as

150

a severe defect in brides. Girls of marriageable age were offered to passing travellers by their own mothers, and wore tokens to show how many lovers they had had. 'And she who has most tokens and can show that she has had most lovers and that most men have lain with her is the most highly esteemed and the most acceptable as a wife; for they say that she is the most favoured by the gods.' It is worth pointing out, in passing, that Marco's frank interest in sexual custom as reflected in the *Travels* shows that he was certainly no prude. 'The country is a fine one to visit for a lad from sixteen to twenty-four,' he concludes – precisely his own age when he was there.

Marco did not like Tibet, however. The place was infested with 'the greatest rogues and the greatest robbers in the world'. It was primitive: salt was the principal means of exchange. True to form, Marco added his customary denigration for such primitive areas, mentioning the 'enchantments' and 'diabolic arts' practised there.

At this point Marco's geography gets decidedly muddled. He next mentions the province of Kaindu to the west, which seems to have been Ning-yuen in Szechwan. Here again, salt was the main form of currency, but in Kaindu the salt was cast in blocks, each imprinted with the Great Khan's stamp. In the whole of this region gold was considerably undervalued, and Marco states that traders from afar could make fortunes there by bartering salt for gold. He probably did himself, as officials of the Great Khan were not forbidden to run their own businesses. Ten days out of Kaindu city he reached the Brius river, which must have been the Kin-sha-kiang, a source of the Yangtse. And across the river lay Marco's goal, Kara-jang, 'a province so large that it contains no less than seven kingdoms'.

Kara-jang (Yunnan province) was ruled over by another of Kubilai's sons, Essen Temur. The first provincial capital Marco reached was Yachi, five days beyond the Brius. Like Kaindu, Yachi did not have a gold-based currency: the chief medium here was gold and cowrie-shells. In Kara-jang province, ten days farther on, gold was found in abundance but the cowries remained the staple currency. Marco noted that the shells were imported from India. Kara-jang province and the city of that name were subject to Hukaji Khan, presumably a younger brother of Essen Temur. Marco took in several unpleasant facts about Kara-jang. First on his list were the horrible 'huge snakes and serpents' which were clearly crocodiles, and the high medicinal value of their gall –

151

according to Marco a cure-all for hydrophobia, labour pains and tumours of any kind.

Marco was also struck by the cruel practice in this region of removing a couple of joints from a horse's tail to stop the animal from swishing its tail – this was considered smart. He also noted that the horsemen of the area rode with long stirrups, European-style, unlike the Tartars who preferred short stirrups on which to stand up and shoot from horseback. Marco then castigates the local practice of using poisoned arrows and cross-bow bolts. 'All the natives, women as well as men, especially those who are bent on evil courses, carry poison about with them.' He adds that it was usual for condemned criminals to try to evade their sentence by taking poison – a practice which the authorities countered by keeping dog's dung at hand. A swift emetic of dog's dung would make the prisoner vomit up the poison. Apart from this unsavoury state of affairs, Marco noted a regional custom which Kubilai's orders had stopped: the habit of murdering guests with fine figures who cast a 'good shadow' – not to rob them, but to give the house the benefit of the strength of the stranger's spirit.

Five days on from Kara-jang Marco reached the westernmost province of the kingdom, Zar-dandan, with its capital city Vochan. Here he was struck by the inhabitants' predilection for complex tattooing and the wearing of ornamental gold cases over the teeth, by the custom of giving new-born babies to the father to look after for forty days ('they say that his wife has had her share of trouble in carrying the infant in her womb') and the fact that here silver was worth five times as much as gold in straight exchange. The locals also used tally-sticks in settling transactions, strips of wood with the appropriate number of notches on both sides, split down the middle, and each party keeping a half. Here was proof of just how much an international aid the tally-stick was for unlettered folk, for at the time tally-sticks were used at the opposite side of the world, as far away as England.

Marco's chief interest in the Vochan area was the fact that a desperate battle had recently been fought there between a Tartar army and an expeditionary force from Burma. Kubilai's expansion from Kara-jang brought him into contact with the powerful 'King of Mien and Bengal'. This un-named potentate had his capital at Pagan on the Irrawaddy, and in 1272 he decided to smash the Tartars in the Vochan area. He marched against the Tartar force of twelve thousand cavalry with a huge force of two thousand war elephants and forty thousand foot and horse. The Tartar general,

Ly dict de la bataille qui fu entre lost et le marescal au grant kaain et le roy de mien.

Et quant le dructeine de lost as tartars sceot certamement que ce roy lui tenoit seure à si grant gent si doubta pour ce que il nauoit que .xij." hommes a chiual. mais sans faille il estoit moult uaillant homme darmes et saiges et acoustumes, z darmes et de bataille. et moult bons dructeine dost. et auoit tro

War elephants, carrying wooden towers for archers. However, in the famous elephant battle in Burma, they were no match for the Tartars. From *Le Livre des Merveilles*.

Chinese Silk Scroll

The Chinese whom Kubilai subdued had a culture of their own which far surpassed any in contemporary Western Europe. The Chinese had already perfected printing techniques, and used paper currency. These details of ink drawing on a silk scroll, 'Spring on the River', dating from the Sung dynasty, show the refinement of Chinese artists of that period.

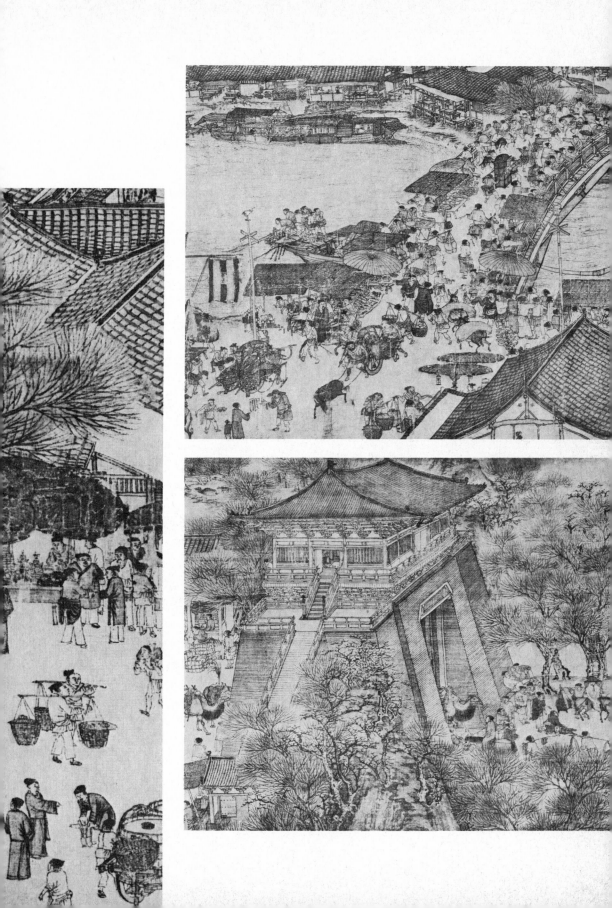

Pagan: this city was the seat
of the Burmese kings from
the eighth century, and was
captured by Kubilai Khan
in 1272 after the elephant battle
described by Marco Polo.

Nasr-uddin, kept his head even when the Tartar horses panicked at the approach of the elephants. He moved back into the wood which he had kept at his back and made his archers fight a dismounted action, breaking up the elephant charge with steady arrow-fire and then taking to horse for a decisive counter-attack which smashed the Burmese army.

Marco's account of the elephant battle is another fairly lengthy interlude in the *Travels*, and this one is slightly different to the others. It reminds us that to a considerable extent Marco was utterly dependent on Messer Rustichello when it came to putting his story into the right words, and that sometimes Rustichello could not resist the temptation to touch up the basic facts with the odd picturesque, conventional phrase as used by the best contemporary romancers and chroniclers. This battle story is also a reminder that by the late thirteenth century in Europe the code of knightly chivalry was taking hold, and that no account of a stand-up fight was complete without due reference to the knightly deeds of arms performed therein. Thus many phrases in the story of the battle with the elephants of Burma could well have been taken from, say, Froissart's account of the battle of Crécy, as the following extract shows. The most obvious examples are in italics:

When the Tartars saw that their horses were so panic-stricken, they dismounted, every one of them, led their mounts into the wood and tethered them to the trees. Then they grasped their bows, fitted their arrows to the string and let fly at the elephants. *They loosed upon them such a shower of arrows that it was truly marvellous*, and the elephants were grievously wounded. Meanwhile the king's men discharged volley after volley against the Tartars in a fierce assault. But the Tartars, who were far stouter combatants than their foemen, defended themselves stubbornly. What need of more words? Be well assured that, when most of the elephants were as sorely wounded as I have told you, they turned in flight towards the king's men *in such a turmoil that it seemed as if the world were tumbling to pieces*. They did not stop until they had reached the woods and then they plunged in and smashed their castles and wrecked and ruined everything. This way and that they hurtled through the woods, goaded to frenzy by their terror. When the Tartars saw this, they did not lose a moment, but sprang to horse and charged down upon the king and his men. They began their attack with arrows; and a deadly onslaught it was, for the king and his men put up a stubborn defence. When all their arrows were shot away, *they set hand to their swords and laid about them lustily, dealing mighty blows. Then you might have seen many a shrewd stroke of sword and club given and received, riders and steeds laid low, hands and arms hewn off and heads severed from their trunks.*

Many there were who fell to earth, dead or wounded to death. So loud was the tumult and the uproar that the thunder of heaven would have gone unheard. Bloody and bitter was the fighting on every side. But never doubt that the Tartars had the better of it. *It was an ill hour for the king and his men when that day's fighting began: so many of them lost their lives in it.* When the battle had lasted till midday and beyond, then the king and his men were in such straits and so many of them slain that they could endure no longer. For it was borne in upon them that if they made any longer stay they would all be dead. So they stayed no longer, but took to flight as best they could. When the Tartars saw that they had turned to flight, *they gave chase with a will, smiting and slaying so grievously that it was pitiful to behold.* . . .

Marco therefore got his view of Burma at the time when the country was still thoroughly cowed by the recent defeat and the swift Tartar follow-up. He adds that the Tartar forces were still engaged in operations on the frontier of 'Bengal', which he places somewhat confusingly *south* of Mien. He is probably referring to the Chittagong/Akyab area west of the Irrawaddy on the coast of the Bay of Bengal.

Marco was enthralled by the wondrous pagodas of the Burmese capital, Pagan, on the River Irrawaddy:

Once a rich and powerful king lived in this city. His dying command was that two towers, one of gold and one of silver, should be built over his tomb or monument. One of these towers was built of fine stone and then sheeted with gold as thick as a finger, so completely covered that it appeared to be made only of gold. It was a full ten paces high, and of a width appropriate to its height. The tower was circular, and all round it were hung small gilded bells which tinkled whenever the wind blew through them. The other tower was plated with silver, but built to the same plan and to the same proportions as the golden one. They were a memorial to the king's greatness, built for the sake of his soul. I can assure you that no fairer towers were to be seen in all the world; they were of indescribable value.'

After marvelling at the beautiful gold-and-silver pagodas of Pagan, and noting that the Tartars had not despoiled them out of their respect for the possessions and monuments of the dead, Marco set off on a roundabout route back to Cathay, east and north-east to Ch'êng-tu-fu and eventually Khanbalig, where he treated Kubilai to a detailed and fascinating report.

Two enduring impressions which Marco picked up on the return journey are conveyed with special detail in the *Travels* and may be quoted here. The first refers to Kaugigu province, east of the

158

Irrawaddy. Once again the subject is tattooing, but this description has such feeling that we may wonder whether or not Marco was tempted to try a small tattoo himself, only to rue the experiment.

All the people, male and female, have their flesh decorated in the following way. They have their flesh covered with pictures of lions and dragons and birds and other objects, printed with needles in such a way that they are indelible. They make these on their faces, their necks, their bellies, their hands, their legs and every part of their bodies. And this is a mark of gentility: the more elaborately anyone is decorated, the greater and the handsomer he is considered. First of all a man will have the images he chooses sketched out in black all over his body. When this is finished they tie him hand and foot, and two or more persons will hold him. Then the artist will take five needles, four of them fastened together in a square and the fifth in the centre, and with these he will work all over his body, pricking out the images previously sketched. As soon as the pricks are made, ink is applied to them and then the figure as sketched appears in the pricks. During the process the victim suffers the equivalent of the pains of Purgatory. Many even die during the operation through loss of blood.

Even further east, in Kuiju province – twelve days out from Ch'êng-tu-fu – the region was infested with 'lions', so badly that 'no one can sleep out of doors at night; for the lions would eat him forthwith'. It is safe to assume that he meant tigers. From his

159

exciting description of how to cope with them, it is even safer to assume that Marco, keen huntsman that he was, took part in the drama of a tiger hunt himself:

When a man is riding along a road with a bow and arrows and two huge dogs and chances upon a full-sized lion, the dogs, which are brave and strong, charge most courageously as soon as they see him, one attacking him in the rear while the other barks in front. The lion rounds upon them; but as fast as he attacks they withdraw so that he cannot touch them, till at last he goes on his way. As soon as the hounds see this, they run after him, snapping at his haunches or his tail. The lion wheels again in a fury but cannot get at them, for they are fast enough to look after themselves. What more shall I say? The lion is scared by the uproar made by the dogs and looks for a tree to guard his back while he faces them. While he retires they keep on biting him in the rear, and he continues to wheel round this way or that. When the hunter sees this, he draws his bow and lets fly an arrow, two arrows and more, until at length the lion falls dead. By this means they kill many; for no lion can defend himself against a mounted man with two good hounds.

Marco's second tour of inspection through Cathay took him off in the opposite direction, south-east through the coastal provinces to the Yangtse and the province of Manzi, until recently the last stronghold of Sung China's resistance to Kubilai. Here was another region about which Kubilai would have been concerned after the anti-Ahmad *coup*, and Marco supplied the details in full measure.

As he journeyed through the peaceful cities of Cathay between Khanbalig and the mouth of the Hwang-ho at Hwai-ngan-chow, Marco's appreciation of the fair sex was particularly enhanced by the Cathayan girls. His coverage of the subject in the *Travels* amounts to a paean of praise:

The girls of Cathay excel in modesty and the strict observance of decorum. They do not frisk or flirt and dance or sulk. They do not watch at the windows gazing at passers-by or inviting their gaze. They do not devour improper stories. They do not gad about to parties and entertainments. When they go out to some respectable place, such as the temples of their idols or to visit the houses of relatives, they walk in the company of their mothers, not gazing brazenly about them but some of them wearing pretty bonnets on their heads which obstruct their upward gaze. In the street they always walk with downcast eyes. In the presence of their elders they are respectful and never utter a needless word – indeed they do not speak at all in their presence unless addressed. . . .

Marco's account of the journey through the home provinces of Cathay south-east of Khanbalig is very streamlined; it is as though

160

he was slightly overwhelmed by the monotony of so much opulence. Three digressions in his text punctuate this stage. The first is his enthusiastic reaction to the Cathayan girls quoted above. The second tells of the skill of the local 'idols' in tracking down lost property via a medium. 'And by this means I, Marco, found a ring that I had lost – but not', he is quick to add for the benefit of European readers, 'by making any offering to the idols or paying them homage.' And this third digression is his account of an earlier Chinese rebellion against Kubilai. This happened in 1262 in Tandinfu province, which Kubilai had entrusted to a Chinese governor, Li-tan. It was a serious affair: 'he consorted with all the leading men of these cities and hatched a plot with them against the Great Khan. And then *with the goodwill of all the inhabitants of the province* [author's italics] they rebelled against the Great Khan and refused them all obedience.' It was not a wise move, for the insurgents could count on only eighty thousand troops, and Kubilai reacted promptly by sending an army of a hundred thousand against them and smashing them in pitched battle. 'All those who were found guilty were put to a cruel death; all the others were pardoned and suffered no harm and never afterwards failed in their loyalty.' Kubilai would have been relieved to hear Marco's account of the tranquillity and prosperity of the former rebel province.

The thesis that Kubilai sent Marco on a detailed inspection tour of southern Cathay, or 'Manzi', as it is called in the *Travels*, is borne out by the way Marco's story suddenly takes on a new lease of life on reaching the Hwang-ho estuary at Hwai-ngan-chow and Kaiju. It is full of details, starting with the account of how the last emperor of Manzi was conquered by Kubilai, and contains one of the most controversial statements in the entire contents of the *Travels*: the assertion that Marco was governor of Yangchow for three years. This has been seriously questioned. Marco's name is not included in the list of governors in Chinese records, and not all the manuscripts of the *Travels* include the claim. Another bone of contention is provided by Marco's account of the siege of Siang-yang-fu, the last Sung city to hold out against Kubilai. Marco states categorically that no progress was made in the siege until the three Polos superintended the construction of a siege battery of three trebuchets, and that a brief bombardment induced the terrified citizens to surrender. 'And the credit for this achievement was due to the good offices of Messer Niccolò and Messer Maffeo and Messer Marco.'

A silver harness ornament
of the Liao dynasty.

This raises the question of what Niccolò and Maffeo were doing
while Marco was touring the Great Khan's provinces. Trading is
one obvious answer, possibly in lucrative customs positions.
Although they were no soldiers, they could certainly have advised
Kubilai to use artillery and given his engineers broad outline
descriptions of how such weapons worked. But it is certain that
all three Polos enjoyed an extensive stay south of the Yangtse.
Marco tells a story connected with the city of Fu-chow, which he
visited at least once in the company of his uncle. Marco and
Maffeo nosed out an underground religious sect which, to their
astonishment, proved to be Christian – a branch of the Christian
faith which had been in China for seven hundred years, and which,
on being granted official toleration by Kubilai on the representation of Marco and Maffeo, turned out to have over 700,000 pro-
fessing families throughout the province of Manzi.

Marco makes it clear, at the end of his account of Manzi, that
he had covered only three of its nine component kingdoms, these
three being Yangchow, Kinsai and Fu-chow. 'Concerning the
others he learned much, but since he did not actually traverse
them, he could not have described them in much detail.' He uses
his experience in Manzi as a bridging passage to introduce the
deep-water port of Zaiton (Amoy), from which he subsequently
embarked on his long voyages south to the East Indies and India –
the route by which the Polos eventually set off for home. And it is

a pity that Marco was not sufficiently intellectually equipped to give us a fuller account of the unique culture of Kinsai (Hangchow), which at that period represented the flower of Chinese civilization in perfect preservation and at the peak of its development.

Hangchow had fallen only in 1270, if 'fallen' is the right word, for the Tartars had not touched it materially. It was the intellectual depository of China, the centre of all matters of the mind. Much more important, it was a records centre where were stored not only every twist of philosophical thought dating back to Confucius but the full spectrum of ancient Chinese poetry and essays. And at Hangchow there were thousands of examples of a phenomenon which no European had ever seen, nor would see for another two centuries, printed books. If Marco was ever shown any, he did not think it sufficiently remarkable to include in the *Travels*. How could he? He was no scholar, let alone a bibliophile. And the worst of it is that at the time that Marco was in Hangchow, the deep concern with ancient Chinese culture had not yet begun to stagnate: it was still at the peak which it had attained under the last of the Sung emperors. All this was lost on Marco. But from his bald account of life in Hangchow we can sense that he did find an aura of splendour and culture there that he had seen nowhere else in Cathay or anywhere else on his travels – an impression that he tried to convey in the only way he knew, a detailed description of the city, its people and their way of life.

The 'City of Heaven', Kinsai. Other travellers in the thirteenth and fourteenth centuries, such as Friar Odoric and Ibn Batuta, endorsed Marco Polo's enthusiasm for the city, the zenith of China's cultural achievement. From *Les Livres du Graunt Caam* (f 257).

The name of the city, Marco states, means 'City of Heaven'. 'It well merits a description, because it is without doubt the finest and most splendid city in the world.' He speaks in his usual style of the size of the city, of its twelve thousand bridges, of its ten huge market-places and the unbelievable amounts of produce and luxuries constantly on sale there. Then the street plan and the city amenities, beginning (with a note of personal appreciation?) with the municipal baths:

In some of these streets there are many cold water baths, with plenty of male and female attendants to look after the men and ladies who go there for a bath; for these people, from childhood upwards, are used to taking cold baths all the time, a habit which they declare to be excellent for the health. But these bath-houses also contain some rooms with hot water for the benefit of foreigners who, not being accustomed to the cold, cannot readily endure it. It is their custom to wash every day, and they will not sit down to a meal without first washing.

Marco was, naturally enough, more taken with the ladies of the town than with the libraries and the learned professors:

These ladies are highly proficient and accomplished in the use of endearments and caresses, with words suited and adapted to every sort of person, so that foreigners who have once enjoyed them are overwhelmed, and so captivated by their sweetness and charm that they can never forget them. So it comes about that, when they return home, they say that they have been in 'Kinsai', that is to say in the city of Heaven, and can scarcely wait to go back there.

The less glamorous attractions of the university quarter are described in one curt sentence: 'In other streets are established the doctors and astrologers, who also teach reading and writing; and countless other crafts have their allotted places round the squares.' In his attempts to convey the magnificence of Hangchow Marco constantly returns to the mercantile theme. He quotes from an official report 'ascertained from an official of the Great Khan's customs'. The first figure which he selects for the amazement of European readers is the amount of pepper consumed daily in Hangchow for the city's own use: forty-three cartloads, 'each cartload consisting of 223 lbs'. Then come the twelve principal trade guilds, each with 'twelve thousand workshops, each employing at least ten men and some as many as forty'.

But the impressive evidence of customs returns and trade figures could not blind Marco to the gracious living favoured by the citizens of Hangchow, and one delightful pastime in particular:

OPPOSITE The Khan presents his golden tablets to Marco, Niccolò and Maffeo Polo. This ensured that they would be provided for and protected by the Khan's subjects as they passed through his territories. From *Les Livres du Graunt Caam* (f 219).

A stoneware pillow with a
drawing of a boy fishing.
Sung dynasty,
twelfth century.

On the southern side of the city there is a lake, some thirty miles round. All round it stand stately palaces and mansions, so magnificent that nothing better or more splendid could be devised or contrived. These are the homes of the nobles and the magnates. There are also abbeys and monasteries of the idolaters in very great numbers. . . .

Besides this, the lake is provided with a great number of boats or barges, big and small, in which the people take pleasure-trips for the sake of recreation . . . anyone who likes to enjoy himself with female society or with his boon companions hires one of these barges, which are kept continually furnished with fine seats and tables and all the other requisites for a party. . . .

And indeed a voyage on this lake offers more refreshment and pleasure than any other experience on earth. On one side it skirts the city, so that the barge commands a distant view of all its grandeur and loveliness, its temples, palaces, monasteries and gardens with their towering trees, running down to the water's edge. On the lake itself is the endless procession of barges thronged with pleasure-seekers. For the people of this

166

LEFT A white glazed spherical porcelain bottle, carved with lotus petals. This piece of Ting ware was excavated at Ting-hsien, Hopei. Sung dynasty, eleventh century.
ABOVE A porcelain ewer and bowl. Sung dynasty, twelfth or thirteenth century.

city think of nothing else, once they have finished the work of their craft or their trade, but to spend a part of the day with their womenfolk or hired women in enjoying themselves either in these barges or in riding about the city in carriages – another pleasure in which, I ought to mention, these people indulge in the same way as they do in boat-trips. For their minds and thoughts are intent upon nothing but bodily pleasures and the delights of society.

Nobody, to be fair, could really blame Marco for concentrating on the delightful pastimes available in Hangchow. All in all, it is the nearest thing to the 'Garden of Earthly Delights' in the whole of the *Travels*. And it is hardly surprising that a man who had crossed the Pamirs and the wastes of the Gobi Desert would find these pleasures much more worth recording than libraries and the intricacies of learned argument. For such is the dominant theme of Marco's description of the 'City of Heaven'. His only trouble is that by the time the reader arrives at this passage in the *Travels*, he

167

وحمد ارغون خان نبرای ضبط اران رسیدهاند اران امیه ولد جنگشا کمد وعلی کلمی وکذکر الحجیان از بندکی قا آن بریدند و آن نیابه اکثری را نغوداشتند و صدر چوب ربین
دبارکه ستوجه الملاق کشته در سراه واردیاب موضع صابی قوربیتای بزرگ ساختند و باز دهم رجب سنه اربع و ثمان ماربه آمد و از انحایم ثلاق اران امیز یحود وحون باران رسیدند یا بعو الملک انشط توز جنائتند که حکم او و امیر عماد الدین
علوی که حکم مریم غار حن حال کی قارس رفید بود کشته ورند ملکان که حوی انشط خون بود بعدانشط شوب کاه یا سار سایند و حکام و حکام فا بر رجب زدند
وحند مد سنه اربع و ثمان سنه و ثمانین اردویا از بندکی قا آن بریدند و ربیع آورد که ارغون نیکای مد زنان ایند و مواحکما کن لقا لناند در ذی دهم صفر
سنه حس و ثمانین و ثمانیه بهرہ یکیا دکر ارغون خان بنخت شاهی نشت و رسم آیین تندمیرسایند و الله اعلم

has been saturated by the limited variety of superlatives in Marco's vocabulary.

Although Marco came out of China without having been impressed by the wealth of printed literature there, one equally famous commodity of the country did catch his eye, porcelain. And he gave it a paragraph to itself.

In a city called Tinju [Fu-chow province] they make bowls of porcelain, large and small, of incomparable beauty. They are made nowhere else except in this city, and from here they are exported all over the world. In the city itself they are so plentiful and cheap that for a Venetian groat you might buy three bowls of such beauty that nothing lovelier could be imagined. These dishes are made of a crumbly earth or clay which is dug as though from a mine. Stacked in huge mounds, it is then left for thirty or forty years exposed to wind, rain and sun. By this time the earth is so refined that dishes made from it are of a pale blue tint with a very brilliant sheen. You must understand that when a man makes a mound of this earth he does so for his heirs; it takes so long to mature that he cannot hope to draw any profit from it himself or to put it to use, but the son who succeeds him will reap the benefit.

It is clear that Marco made several journeys through the coastal provinces of Cathay and Manzi, apart from the unknown official business which kept himself, his father and his uncle there for longer periods. He became familiar with the road to Amoy, the greatest port of Mongol China and at the time arguably the greatest port in the entire world. After proving his worth as a faithful reporter of the Great Khan's most remote dominions by his travels on land, Marco was then entrusted with a mission which took him over half-way home: to India.

8   Back to The West

MARCO'S ACCOUNT OF THE IMMENSE SEA VOYAGES which he made from Cathay while in the Khan's employ are positively infuriating. They are lumped together in the *Travels*; there is no indication of where he went first or what he saw on each voyage. There is only the most casual reference to what he had been sent out for. It is necessary to work backwards to have a chance of getting at the most likely probability. The Polos finally got home because Marco had just got back from a trip to India, and the services of all three were requested by a deputation from the West who wanted to get home by the same route, which led south to Sumatra, through the Singapore Straits, across the Bay of Bengal to Ceylon and thence to Hormuz on the Persian Gulf. In his first trip Marco seems to have covered two-thirds of this route. He got to Ceylon and seems to have taken some time in exploring southern India, some 210 years before Vasco da Gama got there after struggling eastwards round the Cape of Good Hope.

It is typical that the best clue to the reason for Marco's first voyage to the Indies is to be found in a throwaway reference in his passage on Ceylon. There were wonderful relics there, a tooth and begging-bowl attributed to the Buddha himself, and Kubilai wanted them for his collection of religious curios. A treasure fleet was sent out to purchase the relics, and Marco headed the mission.

Marco himself saw Kubilai's reverence for Buddhism at first hand and went so far as to quote the Great Khan's own words on the subject: 'The Christians say that their God was Jesus Christ, the Saracens Mahomet, the Jews Moses and the idolaters Sakya-muni Burkhan, who was the first to be represented as God in the form of an idol. And I do reverence and honour to all four, so that I may be sure of doing it to him who is greatest in heaven and truest; and to him I pray to aid.' Marco had in fact already served as a vehicle for the Great Khan's concern for the collection of relics, by being one of the party which brought the holy oil from Jeru-salem. Now he was to go to Ceylon and bring back Buddha's tooth, and not haggle about the price.

Zaiton – Amoy – was the great port of Cathay. Marco had already seen it during his spell of duty in Manzi and knew it well. He had been powerfully impressed by the ocean-going freighters to be seen in the port: four-masted, with at least sixty cabins, stout hulls of double-thickness planking fastened with nails, with watertight compartments to boot, crews of up to three hundred men and much bigger cargo-carrying capacity than was to be found in contemporary European vessels. We can almost sense

PREVIOUS PAGES The Along coast, near Haiphong, North Vietnam. This photograph shows a typhoon blowing up.

OPPOSITE The Ch'u-fu temple district in the Shantung province of China. Confucius taught there and is buried there.

173

the relief Marco felt in comparing these ships with the leaky
death-traps of Hormuz. But he also noted the weird experiment
which Cathayan seafarers were wont to make before making a
voyage: flying a man-carrying kite with a drunk (or an idiot)
strapped to it. If the kite soared, the voyage would be successful
and safe; if not, 'no merchant will enter this particular ship, because they say that she could not complete her voyage and all sorts
of disasters would overtake her'.

As a natural prelude to the account of the lands which lay on
Cathay's southern sealanes, Marco begins by describing an event
which took place while he was in Cathay and which he may even
have seen at first hand: Kubilai's ill-fated invasion of Japan. In
fact he made two attempts to reduce Japan, both of them failures.
The first had been in 1275, the year of the Polos' arrival in Cathay;
the second was in 1281. Japan was saved only by a cyclone which
smashed up Kubilai's invasion fleet and resulted in heavy losses to
the Tartar expeditionary force. (This storm became enshrined in
Japanese legend as *kamikaze*, the 'Divine Wind' – Japan's
salvation.)

The gist of Marco's description of the voyage from Zaiton to the
Indies begins with the two-month, fifteen hundred-mile crossing
of the China Sea, running down the coast of Manzi to the island of
Hainan and Cochin-China. 'Chamba' – southern Annam – is the
name Marco gives to the region here, and he tells how Kubilai
successfully demanded the submission of the local ruler. Marco
landed here and gives one of his rare dates: 'In the year 1285 I,
Marco Polo, was in this country and at that time this king had
326 children, male and female, including more than 150 men of an
age to bear arms.' Local products: elephants and aloe-wood.
'There are also many groves of the wood called ebony, which is
very black and is used for making chess-men and pen-cases. As
there is nothing else worth noting in our book,' concludes Marco
of this initial stage of the voyage, 'we shall go on our way.'

Next he mentions Java, fifteen hundred miles away to the south-
south-east. Owing to the problem of the long sea approach, Kubilai
had never been able to subdue it. A desirable prize it was, because
it was the centre of the spice trade: 'This is the source of most of
the spice that comes into the world's markets.' Then comes a
description of the lesser islands between Malay and Borneo,
followed by Bintang off the Singapore Strait, and Sumatra, where
Marco had to wait five months 'for weather that would permit us
to continue our voyage' – which presumably means that he got

174

R [adpiez que quant len separt

ABOVE Indian ships arriving
at the port of Zaiton.
From *Les Livres du
Graunt Caam* (f 259v).
OPPOSITE The Wat Po
temple at Bangkok. The
statues are images of Marco
Polo and come from China.

there as the monsoon was breaking. The expedition spent those
five months in a fortified camp on shore 'for fear of these nasty and
brutish folk who kill men for food', but Marco wasted no time in
making a truce with the local cannibals. 'The islanders used to
trade with us for victuals and the like, for there was a compact
between us.' While on Sumatra Marco saw the phenomenon of the
toddy-palm and the wine collected from its lopped branches –
'very good to drink, and a sovereign remedy for dropsy, consump-
tion and the spleen'.

As though a tree which dripped wine were not sufficiently
astonishing for him, Marco encountered another prodigy while on
Sumatra, 'well worthy of note as a marvel', as he says:

You must know that here they have a flour made from trees; and I will
tell you how. There are certain trees here of great height and so thick that
two men join hands round them. After stripping off a thin bark, you reach

176

a layer of wood, perhaps three fingers thick, and inside this is a pith consisting entirely of flour. This flour is put in troughs full of water and stirred with a stick, so that the husks and impurities float to the surface and the pure flour settles on the bottom. Then the water is poured off and the refined flour remains at the bottom of the container. It is then seasoned and made into cakes and various paste dishes, which are exceedingly good. We ourselves often ate them. The wood of these trees is as heavy as iron, and when thrown into water it sinks like iron. This wood can be split in a straight line from top to bottom, like a cane. As I have said, when the tree is emptied of flour, the wood is about three fingers thick. The natives use it for making short lances – not long ones, because if they were long no one would be able to carry them, let alone wield them, owing to the heaviness of the wood. They sharpen the lances at the head and afterwards slightly scorch the point. Lances so treated will surpass any steel-tipped lance in piercing any sort of armour.

Medieval ships in the Java seas, from a bas-relief at Boro Boder. From *The Book of Ser Marco Polo*.

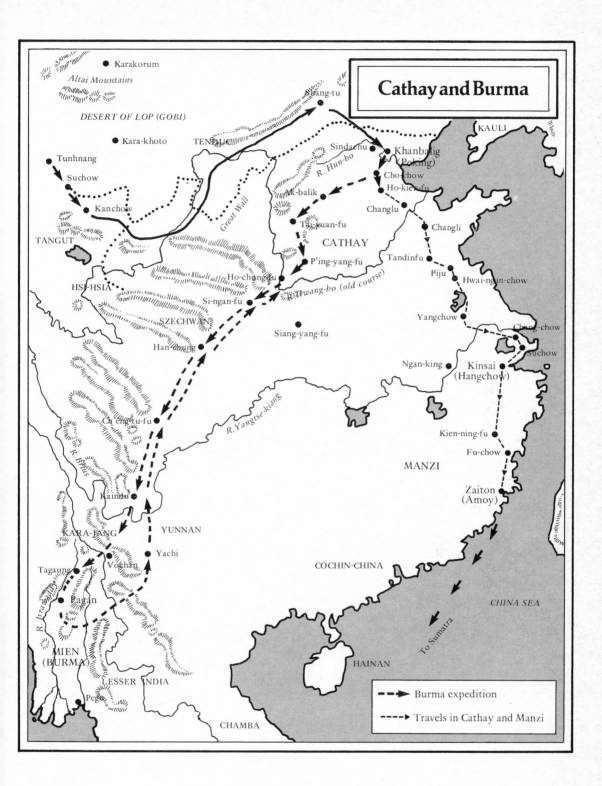

Cathay and Burma

Karakorum

Altai Mountains

DESERT OF LOP (GOBI)

KAULI

Tunhnang

Kara-khoto   TENDUC   Sindachu   Khanbalig
                                    R. Hun-ho   (Peking)

Suchow   Cho-chow

                                    Ak-balik   Ho-kien-fu
Kanchow   Changlu
                              Tai-yuan-fu
TANGUT   Changli
                                    CATHAY
                              P'ing-yang-fu   Tandinfu
HSI-HSIA   Piju
              Ho-chang-fu   Hwai-ngan-chow
                    Si-ngan-fu   *R. Hwang-ho (old course)*
              SZECHWAN   Yangchow
                                                                Chang-chow
              Han-chung   Siang-yang-fu   Suchow

                                                    Ngan-king   Kinsai
                              R. Yangtse-kiang   (Hangchow)

              Ch'eng-tu-fu
                                                    Kien-ning-fu
R. Brius   Fu-chow

                                                    MANZI
              Kaindu
                                                    Zaiton
              KARA-JANG   (Amoy)
                         YUNNAN
Tagaung   Vochan   Yachi
                                   COCHIN-CHINA

R. Irrawaddy   Pagan   *CHINA SEA*

MIEN   *To Sumatra*
(BURMA)
         LESSER INDIA   HAINAN
                    Pegu

                         CHAMBA

- - -► Burma expedition

- - - Travels in Cathay and Manzi

Thus, out of his five-month sojourn on Sumatra, Marco emerged with his own account – the first recorded by a European witness – of a dish which has since depressed generations of children: sago.

When the voyage was resumed, north-westward from Sumatra, the next major landfall was in the Nicobar Islands, followed by the Andamans. Marco wrote off the inhabitants of both archipelagos as the rock-bottom of civilization. 'They have no king, and the people live like wild beasts,' he notes crushingly. And then came the straight east-west crossing of the Bay of Bengal, a thousand miles in all, to Ceylon itself, about which Marco waxes lyrical – 'un-doubtedly the finest island of its size in all the world'. The reader of the *Travels* has to hop backwards and forwards to gather all Marco's impressions of Ceylon. He saw the place at least three times – the first landfall after the Andamans, on returning from India, and finally on the journey home – and this obviously rubbed off when he came to describe it.

Back in Persia Marco had been excited when he visited the tomb of the Three Magi, and this excitement bubbled up again in the religious legends which he absorbed in Ceylon. First were the stories connected with Adam's Peak in the centre of the island – 'It is said that on the top of this mountain is the monument of Adam, our first parent.' But it also seems clear that in his quest for the tooth of the Buddha, Marco had done some research on the customs of the 'idolaters' and had been profoundly impressed by links with Christian tradition. The story of 'Sakyamuni Burkhan' – Gautama – he considered worthy of quotation in full, because of its similarity with the life of St Josaphat, another spoiled young prince who chose discipline and privation as a clue to the mysteries and suffering of this world. Ceylon was the traditional burial-place of Sakyamuni, and his teeth and begging-bowl were there. Marco states that Kubilai sent his mission to seek these relics in 1284, the date we need to confirm that Marco himself was the mission's leader. The quest was successful and the relics eventually found their way back to Kubilai at Khanbalig. 'What they cost him in treasure amounted to no small sum,' Marco added, but Kubilai was overjoyed. He 'welcomed them with great joy and great ceremony and great reverence'.

Although this part of the mission was successfully carried out, Marco was unable to purchase another rarity which Kubilai had wanted. This was the biggest ruby in the world, and was both the prized family heirloom and totem of the ruling kings of Ceylon. Clearly it was a prodigious jewel: 'about a palm in length and of the thickness of a man's arm. It is the most brilliant object to behold in the world, free from any flaw and glowing red like fire.' The contents of Kubilai's treasure fleet availed Marco nothing; this wonderful jewel, he was plainly told, was not for sale at any price.

After completing the Great Khan's business in Ceylon, Marco crossed to India and obviously travelled extensively in the states of the Deccan Peninsula, but here again his shaky geography causes many doubts as to where he actually went. The first Indian state he mentions is the 'great province' of Maarbar, across the strait from Ceylon. These waters were world-famous for pearl fishing, and Marco describes the entire process in detail.

A group of merchants will band together to form a partnership and will take a large ship specially adapted for the purpose, in which each will have a handy cabin fitted for his use containing a tub of water and other requisites. There will be a great many such ships, because there are many merchants who devote themselves to this sort of fishery. And all the merchants who are associated in one ship will have several boats to tow her through the gulf. It is their practice to hire men for a certain sum for the month of April and half of May; for that is the local fishing season. The place where pearls are most plentiful is called Betala, and is on the mainland. From there they sail out for sixty miles towards the south and there anchor. Then they go out in small boats and begin to fish in the following way. The men in the small boats, who have been hired by the merchants, jump overboard and dive into the water, sometimes three fathoms down, sometimes four, sometimes as much as ten. They stay under as long as they can. When they can endure no longer, they come to the surface, rest a short while and then plunge in again; and so they continue all day. While they are at the bottom, they gather there certain shells which are called sea oysters. In these oysters are found pearls, big and small and of every variety. The shells are split open and put into the tubs of water of which I have spoken. The pearls are embedded in the flesh of the shell-fish. In the water this flesh decays and takes on the appearance of the white of egg. In this form it floats to the surface, while the pearls divested of impurities remain at the bottom. That is how the pearls are gathered. And I assure you that the quantities gathered are beyond counting. For you must know that pearls gathered in this gulf are exported throughout the world, because most of them are round and lustrous. In the middle of May this fishing stops, because the pearl-bearing shells are no longer to be found. But it is a fact that about three hundred miles away they are found in September and in the early half of October.

From all this detail it is fair to suppose that Marco formed part of a

A statue near Madras said to have been brought to Madras by St 'Doubting' Thomas. This shrine commemorates his death as a missionary in India.

pearl-fishing syndicate at some time during his travels out of Cathay, with rich benefit to the pooled treasure of the Polos. Certainly, jewel-fever is very noticeable at this point in the *Travels*. Of Maarbar itself he was struck by the fact that the people went about stark naked, even the king, who must have been an impressive sight because he was loaded with beautiful jewellery from head to foot.

Among the many 'marvels' which made up Marco's memories of Maarbar were the Brahman priests, the worship of cattle, *suttee* (the burning-alive of the widow on her husband's funeral pyre) and the gruesome spectacle of fanatics mutilating themselves in public and finally cutting off their own heads out of devotion to their god. Maarbar was also notable in that there St Thomas the

182

Apostle – 'Doubting Thomas' – had ended his life. Marco tells how the saint was praying in the wood near his hermitage, and was hit by an arrow fired by a hunter aiming at a peacock. 'And when he had received the blow he worshipped his creator most fervently, and of that blow he died.'

North of Maarbar Marco came to Motupalli, ruled over in his time by a wise widow queen – 'never was lady or lord so well beloved as she is by her subjects'. But her land was noted for its fabulous diamonds, and Marco noted the current legends about these stones. 'In all the world diamonds are found nowhere else except in this kingdom alone . . . you must not suppose that diamonds of the first water come to our countries of Christendom. Actually they are exported to the Great Khan and to the kings and noblemen of these various regions and realms, for it is they who have the wealth to buy all the costliest stones.' Diamond-trading, therefore, was certainly a subsidiary part of Marco's mission after securing the sacred teeth from Ceylon.

While on the subject of diamond prospecting, Marco comes up with a story which is in startling contrast to the accuracy of his observations of the pearl fisheries. It reads like something straight out of the *Arabian Nights*:

These mountains are so infested with snakes of immense size and thickness that men cannot go there without grave danger. Let me tell you further that these snakes are exceedingly venomous and dangerous, so that men dare not venture into the caves where the serpents live. So they get the diamonds by other means. You must know that there is a big deep valley so walled in by vertical cliffs that no one can enter it. But I will tell you what men do. They take many lumps of raw meat dripping with blood and fling them down into the depths of the valley. And the lumps thus flung down pick up great numbers of diamonds, which become stuck in the flesh. Now it so happens that these mountains are inhabited by a great many white eagles, which prey on the snakes. When these eagles spot the meat lying at the bottom of the valley they swoop down and seize the lumps and carry them off. The men observe attentively where the eagles go, and as soon as they see that a bird has alighted and is swallowing the meat, they rush to the spot as fast as they can. Scared by their sudden approach, the eagles fly away, leaving the meat behind. And when they get hold of it, they find plenty of diamonds sticking in it. Another means by which they get the diamonds is this. When the eagles eat the meat they also swallow the diamonds. Then at night, when the eagle comes back, it deposits the diamonds with its droppings. So men run and collect these droppings, and find diamonds in plenty.

Trivandrum: India's
southernmost tip.

184

So Marco's memories of India continue to jostle each other in the pages of the *Travels*: coconut-palms and sago-trees, Brahmans and *yogis*, wonder after wonder to Europeans of his day, but to us presented in the most confusing form. There is no indication of when he finally left India and set off on the long sea voyage back to Cathay with the relics and riches collected on the journey. For the next positive date in Marco's life we have to turn to the domestic history of the ilkhanate of Persia, and yet another mission which at last offered the Polos the chance to get home.

It is clear that by about 1286 the Polos were on the point of accepting that Kubilai would never let them go. Time and again he had evaded their requests, and the only hope they must have had was that Kubilai was now an old man. Then, in about 1288, messengers arrived in Khanbalig from the West. They came from the Court of Arghun, Ilkhan of Persia. His Queen, Bolgana, had died, her last wish being that Arghun's next wife should be a member of her own royal clan. An embassy was sent off from Persia to Cathay by the overland route – its arrival there probably took place while Marco was still sailing back to Zaiton from the Indies. Kubilai approved the selection of a suitable bride for his great-nephew, a seventeen-year-old princess called Kokachin. In 1289 the bridal party set off, again by the overland route, on the return journey to Persia. But after eight months they had to turn back: a Tartar war had broken out and the road was effectively barred. So back they went to Khanbalig to seek Kubilai's aid.

When the discomforted Persian envoys and their young charge reached Kubilai's capital, Marco had just returned from his trip to India. The ceremonial reception of the sacred teeth was followed by another of Marco's detailed reports about where he had been. We can imagine the Persian envoys listening with growing interest to this account, and realizing that here was probably the best hope they had of carrying out their mission. The elder Polos, for their part, had not overlooked the return of the Persians and came to an agreement with them in private. The upshot was that Kubilai was soon faced with a joint deputation: the Persian envoys and the three Polos. As Marco's Prologue has it:

They went to the Great Khan and begged him as a favour to send them home by sea and to let the three Latins accompany them. The Great Khan, who was very fond of the three, as I have told you, granted this request with some reluctance and gave leave to the three Latins to travel with the three lords and the lady.

When the Great Khan saw that Messer Niccolò and Messer Maffeo and Messer Marco were ready to leave, he ordered all three to be brought into his presence. He then gave them two tablets proclaiming that they might travel freely throughout his realm, and that wherever they went they should receive provisions for themselves and their attendants. He entrusted them with a message for the Pope and the kings of France and Spain, and the other kings of Christendom. Then he fitted out a fleet of fourteen ships. . . .

For all parties concerned this must have been a period of tangled but powerful emotions. As far as the three Polos were concerned, homesickness had finally got the upper hand and they would have been tense with apprehension that Kubilai might after all change his mind at the last minute. As for Kubilai, he seems to have given in with good grace to the departure of the three men of whom he had grown genuinely fond and whom he was going to miss badly. Generous as ever, he gave his parting guests a fleet which would enable them to take away as much of their wealth as possible – fourteen of the big freighters described by Marco would have carried an emperor's ransom by European standards. Kubilai gave them his famous passports, and equipped them with the lavish retinue befitting Tartar lords. Two years' worth of provisions were provided for the voyage. The moment of departure finally came.

Considering the flashes of dramatic detail which Marco did include in his book, it can only be a matter for profound regret that he did not think fit to describe the Polos' leave-taking with the Great Khan. It would have been a moment of great emotion and great dignity. We are not told for certain, but it is hard to imagine Kubilai, despite his age, not travelling with the Polos to Zaiton when the party left Khanbalig for the last time.

As the fleet put out to sea and shaped its course to the south, both sides knew that they would never see each other again.

9 Home

I T ALMOST GOES WITHOUT SAYING that Marco failed to provide a full account of his long and eventful journey home. This is particularly unfair, because in the Prologue he drops plenty of hints that it was a dramatic affair. It took the party twenty-one months to get to the Persian Gulf. In that time 582 of the party died – but Marco does not give the remotest clue as to what went wrong on the trip. Once again we have to turn back to his overall description of the East Indies and India, and wonder how many of these experiences can be assigned with any accuracy to the first or the second journey there.

The Polos and the Persian envoys had a considerable responsibility. Princess Kokachin was not the only worry: the party included 'the daughter of the king of Manzi', no less than a Sung princess. The two ladies were attended by a hundred ladies-in-waiting.

Marco says that it took the fleet three months to get to 'Java', by which he obviously means Sumatra. It is unlikely that anything serious happened to the party during this phase; Sumatra, however, was another matter. It is quite possible that the five-month delay on Sumatra to which Marco alludes in his description of the Indies occurred on this return trip. We know that the natives were hostile. There is a case for imagining the Polos besieged in camp and having to fight off repeated attacks to defend their charges. This would certainly help to explain the tremendous mortality among the six hundred men with whom the party had sailed. If this was the case, the ladies were well defended, for only one of the ladies-in-waiting died on the entire journey.

From the sequence of Indian provinces and kingdoms as they appear in Marco's description of India, it is easier for us to reconstruct the homeward voyage after the surviving ships quitted Ceylon. Marco mentions Comorin, on the western side of the tip of the Deccan, as the place 'in which it first becomes possible to see the Pole Star, which we have not seen all the way since we left Java'. Then comes Ely, three hundred miles further up the Malabar coast; a description of the kingdom of Malabar itself; then Thana, Cambay, Somnath and finally Kech-Makran. A glance at the map shows that this sequence indicates a course which would have been seldom out of sight of land, coasting along the western shore of the Indian sub-continent past the modern frontier of West Pakistan. After Kech-Makran the next landfall mentioned by Marco is the familiar name of Hormuz.

All this makes sense, and can be taken to indicate the route

Marco Polo disembarks at
Hormuz on the return
journey. From *Le Livre
des Merveilles*.

which the Polos and the princesses actually followed.

While describing the major landfalls along the coast of western India, Marco mentions two dangers to seaborne travellers which might also offer a very good clue to the losses suffered by the Polos' fleet. Ths first occurs during his brief description of the kingdom of Ely:

In this province or kingdom there is no port, apart from a big river with an excellent estuary. . . . Any ship that enters the estuary and sails upstream, if it is not a ship that is bound for this place, they seize it and take over the whole cargo. They say: 'You were bound elsewhere and God has sent you to me, so that I may take all that you have.' Then they seize all the goods in the ship and keep them for their own and do not consider that they have done anything wrong. This practice is followed throughout all these provinces of India. If any ship is driven by bad weather to put in at any place other than its proper destination, it is seized the moment it comes ashore and robbed of everything on board. For the inhabitants will say: 'You meant to go somewhere else; but my good luck and merit have brought you here, so that I should have all your possessions.'

As Marco gives many examples of his laconic attitude to personal danger elsewhere in the *Travels*, this passage could quite reasonably be taken to refer to an incident on the return journey, when the Polos sent in one of their ships to find a good anchorage and it was overwhelmed by the locals on approaching the shore. A fight to get it back would then have ensued, and such trouble could have occurred more than once, from what Marco says. This would certainly explain the heavy toll in the manpower of the fleet by the time it arrived at Hormuz.

But Marco mentions another danger which makes even more sense – pirates. He gives such detail on their technique that it amounts to a suggestion that the fleet was attacked at sea.

Marco says that the ports of the Malabar and Gujarat coasts harboured pirate fleets that sailed every year, up to a hundred strong, to plunder merchant shipping along the Indian coast. He lays stress on the scale of their depredations; they took their wives and children to sea with them and terrorized the coastal sealane all summer. Sometimes they would prowl independently; sometimes they would act with naval precision, stringing out into a patrol-line with about five miles in between each ship, so that a pirate fleet of twenty vessels could sweep a hundred miles of sea. As soon as a likely victim was sighted the whole fleet would be alerted by means of beacon signals passed down the line, making it virtually impossible for a merchant ship to get through unde-

194

tected. With such a danger facing them the merchants used to sailing those waters had got into the habit of putting to sea armed to the teeth – rather like the big merchantmen of the East India Company in its heyday – and were therefore ready to beat off attack if necessary. Even so, it was impossible to save every merchant ship and every now and then one was bound to be snapped up by the pirates. An interesting point: 'When the pirates capture a ship, they help themselves to both ship and cargo; but they do not hurt the crew. They say to them: "Go and fetch another cargo. Then, with luck, you may bring us some more."'

Marco moves on from this goose-that-lays-the-golden-egg attitude on the part of the pirates to a singularly unpleasant trick of theirs, one practised particularly by the raiders from the Gujarat coast. When these pirates captured merchants they would force their hapless victims to drink an emetic of tamarind and seawater, inducing copious vomiting. It was not a torture, but an additional search. Once the vomit hit the deck it was then carefully picked apart by the pirates to see if it contained pearls or gems hastily swallowed to prevent capture. Marco may have heard of this revolting but doubtless effective trick from a merchant who had had it done to him, while gathering information on the dangers of the waters which the Polos' fleet would have to traverse.

But as though he wanted deliberately to confuse his readers, Marco includes a bewildering chapter in which he describes the main landmarks of the entire Arabian Sea, including the East African coast as far south as Zanzibar and Madagascar! As it is almost impossible to imagine the party visiting all these places – especially in the order mentioned – it is best to accept that Marco's final description of the Indian Ocean was made from the perspective of Hormuz, before the party moved inland on the last stage of its journey.

He starts with a mystery: 'Male' and 'Female' Islands, out in the Arabian Sea, 'five hundred miles south of Kech-Makran'. We are not helped by the knowledge that Marco's compass bearings are erratic, to say the least. He describes the population of these twin islands somewhat confusingly as 'baptized Christians, observing the rule and customs of the Old Testament'. According to Marco, the islands were thirty miles apart and got their names because the men lived on one island and the women on the other. 'Visiting time' for the men was restricted to three months a year: March, April and May; as soon as boy children reached the age of fourteen they were sent to join the menfolk on Male Island.

The fabulous gryphon-bird that snatched up elephants and burst them on the rocks below. From a Persian drawing reproduced in *The Book of Ser Marco Polo*.

Next on Marco's list is the island of Socotra, five hundred miles to the south. This he describes as a centre for whaling, but one with the strangest methods. The whale is lured with portions of drugged tunny-fish and rendered incapable of escape; the whalers then row alongside and hammer the harpoon into the whale's head with a mallet. Two other facts about Socotra, as noted by Marco, stand out: the archbishop of Socotra was appointed by an eastern archbishop at Baghdad, not by the Pope of Rome; and the island was a wealthy trading-centre for pirates.

From Socotra Marco's description takes a thousand-mile leap southward to Madagascar, which, he states firmly, represents the southernmost 'point of no return' for shipping. 'Ships cannot sail to the other islands that lie farther south, because the current sets so strongly towards the south that they would have little hope of returning.' With perfect seriousness, but stressing that it is a second-hand story, Marco goes on to tell of the gryphon-birds of the southern islands that are so big that they feed on elephants, dropping the unfortunate pachyderms from a great height and gorging on the burst carcasses. He also mentions that envoys from the Great Khan had returned from these islands with the tusks of a gigantic boar – 'they declare that some of these boars are as big as

196

buffaloes'. For the explorers of Marco's day – and for centuries after him – the Sinbad-the-Sailor fantasy of gryphon-birds went naturally with the reality of hippopotami.

Zanzibar was covered next, 'a large and splendid island some two thousand miles in circumference'. Marco was not taken with the heavily-built Negroes of Zanzibar, each of whom, according to him, was strong enough to do the work of four normal men and ate enough for five. He also found the local women physically repulsive. Zanzibar was, in Marco's time, a centre for ivory trading. He also says that the inhabitants used elephants in battle, and adds the singular fact that they got their elephants drunk on wine before joining battle. 'They do this because, when an elephant has drunk this wine, he grows more ferocious and mettlesome and acquits himself proportionately better in battle.'

With Zanzibar, Marco completed his account of the islands of the Indian Ocean, breezily assuring the reader that according to the maps and records of his time there were no less than 12,700 islands in the Indian Ocean, both inhabited and uninhabited. He then turned his attention to the mainland shores of the Indian Ocean, beginning with Abyssinia. Opening with the somewhat startling statement that Abyssinia is in 'Middle India', he says that it is made up of six subordinate kingdoms. Three of these are Christian, three Moslem, but the balance is held by the high king, who is Christian. St Thomas, on his way to Maarbar and his death from the peacock-hunter's arrow, preached in Abyssinia. Marco tells a story to illustrate the constant feuding between the Christians of Abyssinia and the Moslems of the sultanate of Aden. The high king of Abyssinia wished to go on pilgrimage to Jerusalem, but was argued out of it by his lords and sent a bishop in his stead. The bishop completed his pilgrimage and headed for home, but was captured by the sultan of Aden on the way. The sultan told the bishop to embrace Islam or die, and when the bishop chose death, he was circumcised and released, to show his master what the sultan thought of him. The king of Abyssinia was naturally incensed and led an army against Aden in revenge. The story ends with a catalogue of bloodthirsty deeds of valour wrought by the Christian army so vicious and chauvinistic in its scorn of the 'Saracen dogs' that one wonders how much of it consists of Marco's own words. A note of general tolerance underlines his references to the myriad cults, creeds and faiths he encountered in the Far East. A cynic might claim that this sudden vicious tone was the result of Marco's return to European civilization.

After Abyssinia, the sultanate of Aden itself and its natural eminence at the mouth of the Red Sea. Aden was to the Red Sea what Hormuz was to the Persian Gulf, a crossroads of trade. Aden was the natural funnel for the imports of Mamluk Egypt and for the export of Arab horses to India, and its rulers took full advantage of the fact. 'I assure you that the Sultan of Aden derives a very large revenue from the heavy duties he levies from the merchants coming and going in his country. Indeed, thanks to these, he is one of the richest rulers in the world.' There is another touch of unwarranted resentment in Marco's reference to the help which the Sultan of Aden gave to the Mamluks in finally wresting Acre from the Christians. 'And this he did more from ill will to the Christians than from any good will to the Sultan of Egypt or from any love he bears him.'

Memories of the Polos' earlier horror at the unseaworthy state of the ships of Hormuz and the Gulf are revived by Marco's reference to the use of inflated skin life-rafts in those waters.

After finishing his account of Aden, Marco ticks off the main landmarks heading eastwards round the coast of Arabia: Shihr, Dhofar and Kalhat, the latter port lying three hundred miles south-south-east of Hormuz. And it was to Hormuz that the survivors of the Polos' fleet came after completing their coasting voyage along the coast of India from Ceylon. After the perils of the sea voyage from Cathay, they might have been excused for feeling a sense of relief at finding themselves once more in comparatively familiar territory. But their troubles were by no means over. The Tartar wars in Turkestan, which had forced the original overland mission to turn back to Khanbalig, were in fact a symptom of the growing turbulence within the once stable khanates of the Mongol Empire. The stability which had helped the Polos to cross Persia over eighteen years before was a thing of the past. For Arghun Khan, whose young bride had been the unwitting medium by which the Polos had finally disengaged themselves from Kubilai's hospitality, was dead. Persia was threatened by a disputed succession, civil war and invasion from without.

The Polos must have cursed Hormuz as never before. This was the second time they had arrived at the wretched place to find their plans wrecked. But the Polos' resilience had not been affected by their long stay at Kubilai's Court. They sought for the new ruler and found that Arghun had been illegally succeeded by his brother Kaikhatu. The next move was to send a message to Kaikhatu and ask what was to be done with the princesses. Kaikhatu's verdict

An Ethiopian sheep illustrated in *The Book of Ser Marco Polo*.

was that Princess Kokachin should be given in marriage to Arghun's son, Prince Ghazan. The latter was on the northern marches of Persia, in the region of the Dry Tree; he was keeping watch on Persia's north-east frontier to prevent any neighbouring power from attempting to exploit Persia's current weakness by raids or invasion.

The news of Ghazan's whereabouts must have affected the Polos in a singular manner. For over twenty years they had been roaming the world. And now, as they set off from Hormuz to find Ghazan, they were covering the same road as they had used on their outward journey, having completed a gigantic oval in their return to Hormuz by sea.

In due course the Polos arrived at Ghazan's camp. Marco describes the Prince as being on the horns of a dilemma, thirsting to march against his usurping uncle and recover his rightful throne, but pinned to his watch over the frontier by an overriding sense of duty. Princess Kokachin was duly presented, and the Polos prepared to take their leave. It was an emotional parting, for the three Polos had become deeply fond of the girl during the long voyage and the affection was mutual. In his Prologue Marco says that she had come to look on them with the trust of a daughter, and that she wept when they finally left. But apparently there was a happy ending for the couple; Ghazan finally recovered his throne in 1294, and the marriage turned out to be a happy one.

One unsolved point in the story is the eventual fate of the unnamed Sung princess whom the Polos had brought from Cathay with Kokachin. She simply vanishes from the narrative. She is a pathetic if anonymous figure: the heiress to one of the oldest reigning houses the world had seen, uprooted from a life of peace and culture in her native land and carried to oblivion in the turbulence of the West.

After leaving Kokachin in Ghazan's care, the Polos returned to the Court of Kaikhatu. Marco does not say precisely where this was, but it must have been somewhere between Tabriz and Isfahan – west of the Caspian – 'because that was the direction in which their road lay'. Kaikhatu seems to have been a realist, despite the murky reputation which Marco gives him. He respected the Polos' status as envoys of the Great Khan and gave them new golden passports of his own to see the travellers safely through his western provinces in safety. Marco admits that the passports were powerful enough. 'Throughout his dominions they [the Polos] were supplied

Persian silver inlaid bowls with engraved inscriptions: eleventh- or twelfth-century.

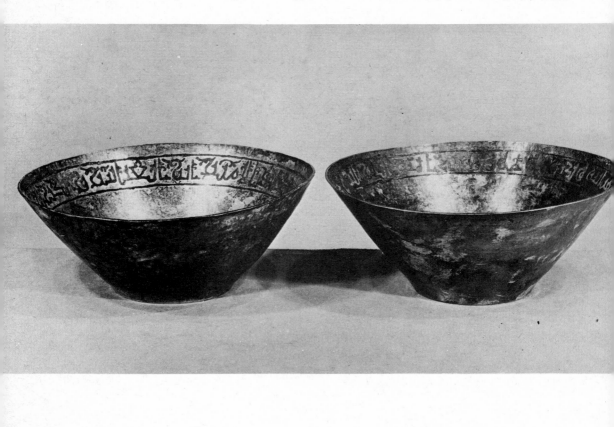

with horses and provisions and everything needful, and that in great plenty. I assure you for a fact that on many occasions they were given two hundred horsemen, sometimes more and sometimes less, according to the number needed to escort them and ensure their safe passage from one district to another.'

It was probably during this last crisis in Persia that Marco gathered material for a special chapter in the *Travels* which is given a section all to itself. Although it deals mainly with Tartar wars in general, the dominant theme is the House of Persia and how everything eventually came right with the accession of Ghazan.

The first Tartar leader to emerge in this chapter was the rebel nephew of Kubilai, Kaidu Khan, overlord of Samarkand in Turkestan. After describing Kaidu's arrogant independence and acts of defiance against Kubilai, Marco tells of the greatest Tartar battle fought in his time. This took place between the army of Kaidu and one led by Numughan, a son of Kubilai, and Prince George, none other than the grandson of Prester John himself. A battle was fought in the heart of Mongolia, near Karakorum, in 1269. It was a head-on collision, and the action was fought to a bloody draw.

A Persian bronze basin inlaid with silver: twelfth-century.

De lestoille de mer.

Ette estoille de mer qui ne senuut ſ
voit vne autre au contraire de eſtel
les marinues deycela par eſte eſto
quelle napert point a nous. et eſto
voint a culr. vourquoy on met e

LEFT Sailing ships in the
Andamans. From *Le Livre
des Merveilles*.
ABOVE Fishing for pearls in
the gulf of Malabar. From *Les
Livres du Graunt Caam* (f 265).

Both armies gave their all in desperate efforts to defeat the enemy. But all to no purpose. The fighting lasted till evening, but neither army had managed to drive the other from the field. . . .

When morning broke, Kaidu the king, who had received news that the Great Khan was sending a mighty host to attack him, made up his mind that he would do ill to tarry. So in the first light of dawn he and his troops armed themselves, mounted their horses and set out on their homeward journey. When the Great Khan's son and Prester John's grandson saw them go, they were too worn and weary for pursuit but let them go in peace.

The story passes to Kaidu's daughter, Princess Aiyaruk — 'Bright Moon'. She displayed an independence which must have warmed her father's heart. 'She was so strong that in all the kingdom there was no squire or gallant who could vanquish her. But I assure you that she used to vanquish them all. The king her father wished to give her a husband. But she steadfastly refused, declaring that she would never take a husband till she found some nobleman who could get the better of her in a trial of strength.' Despite wide advertisement and a ready supply of eager suitors, this formidable lady remained unbeaten against the toughest wrestlers who cared to try their luck with her. Marco concludes: 'King Kaidu took this same daughter of his into many battles. And in every affray there was never a knight more doughty than she. For many a time it happened that she plunged in among the enemy and seized a knight by force and carried him off into her own ranks.' And on this note the iron-muscled wrestling princess disappears from history.

Marco's account of the Tartar wars then turns west and takes up the story of Arghun, son of Abaka Khan. Arghun apparently entered public life in Persia as commander of the frontier patrol army in the region of the Dry Tree. In this position he decisively repulsed an attack against him by an army led by Kaidu Khan's brother, Barak. But on the death of his father, Abaka, Arghun was forced into civil war by the treasonable seizure of the throne by his uncle Ahmad, who had turned Moslem.

Marco's account then changes style so considerably that it seems obvious that Rustichello took over again for the final draft of this passage. It breaks into an almost conscious parody of current European chronicle-styles, with formal challenges, eve-of-battle speeches and general ornamentation. All ended well for Arghun, with Ahmad being hunted down and killed 'and his body flung into some place where no one ever found it'.

All this Tartar history Marco obviously considered necessary to bring the story up to date:

When Arghun was established once more in the chief palace in full enjoyment of his lordship, all the barons from every part who had been subject to Abaka his father came to do homage to him as their lord and obeyed him as they should. And Arghun sent Ghazan his son with some thirty thousand horsemen to the district of the Dry Tree to protect his land and people. And this recovery of the lordship by Arghun occurred in the year of Our Lord 1286. Ahmad Sultan held the lordship for two years, and Arghun reigned for six years. At the end of this time he died of an illness, though rumour has it that he was poisoned.

It was shortly after this that the Polos finally turned up at Hormuz to find that the Princess Kokachin no longer had a bridegroom waiting for her, until Ghazan appeared as a substitute.

So it was that the Polos quitted Persia for the last time, heading back to the country where their outward journey had started, Armenia. This time, however, they did not make for the Mediterranean, as the elder Polo had done so long ago in 1269. They made for the eastern end of the Black Sea and the port of Trebizond, and took ship for Constantinople. There they embarked for Negropont, and from Negropont, at long last, they arrived in Venice in 1295.

After twenty-three years it was hardly surprising that their arrival at home caused something of a stir. Certainly the stories which grew up around the return of the Polos are still famous – how their barbarous Tartar clothing caused them to be turned away as tramps, but how distrust turned to wonder when they ripped open the seams of their robes and sent clattering streams of jewels raining on to the table as proof of their *bona fides*. There is certainly no indication that the Polos did *not* come home wealthy from the Far East, despite the dangers of the journey.

We know for certain of only one more dramatic episode in Marco Polo's life: he was captured in a sea battle during a war between Venice and Genoa, in which he seems to have taken part as the 'gentleman commander' of a Venetian galley. The date of this has been hotly disputed, but it was between 1296 and the battle of Curzola, which the Genoese won in September 1298. One fact is certain: he was temporarily imprisoned in Genoa, and while he was imprisoned, he and Rustichello of Pisa collaborated to produce the first version of the *Travels*. Marco himself was released in May 1299, by which time the book was finished, and it first appeared in Venice soon afterwards.

205

A document dated 1305 gives us the nickname which Marco had already been given: *il Milione*, or 'Marco Millions'. And then, dated 9 January 1323–4, there is his Will, leaving his wealth (by no means a super-fortune by then) to his three daughters. Of his wife we know nothing. It is clear from his own account that he had travelled around the shores of the Black Sea and penetrated into southern Russia; the *Travels* contain references to the murderous cold of the Russian winter, which the inhabitants countered with huge stoves and vodka. It is quite possible that when Marco settled down to peaceful trading, he proved less successful (or had less amazing luck) than his father and uncle, and suffered a run of heavy losses. But this, too, is only guesswork.

Marco Polo was seventy years old when he died. Few if any men or women have ever seen as much as he did in his allotted 'three score and ten'. Many famous men have had memorable dying words attributed to them, but those for which Marco is

ABOVE Marco Polo's galley enters the battle of Curzola. A print used in Yule's *The Book of Ser Marco Polo*.
LEFT Marco Polo dictating his story to Messer Rustichello in his cell in Genoa. From the first edition of Yule's book.

Marco Polo's last Will, a facsimile reproduced in Yule's *The Book of Ser Marco Polo*.
OPPOSITE Campo San Lorenzo, where Marco Polo died.

remembered have always been accepted – justly – as a perfect epitaph for him.

The story goes that his friends urged the dying man to take back some of the most obvious exaggerations he had made about his experience, lest he meet his Maker with lies on his conscience. To which Marco murmured: 'I never told the half of what I saw. . . .'

10 Achievement

MARCO POLO'S ENDURING MONUMENT, obviously, is his book of travels, one of the most remarkable ever written. He was not a writer himself, and the *Travels* would not have appeared at all in the form which we know today had it not been for his providential meeting with Rustichello while in the hands of the Genoese. Anyone reading it will agree that this is something of a pity – certainly so far as Marco's own story is concerned. All the detective-work involved in trying to follow Marco's footsteps cannot guarantee that a clear and accurate story will emerge. But I submit that the version given in the previous chapters is as viable as any other which has been put forward. There are quite enough unsolved questions about Marco's story without overlaying them with learned temporizing and a frustrating scatter of 'verdicts unproven'.

For example, it is hard to believe that Marco relied exclusively on his memory when it came to writing the *Travels*. If he really did, he must have been one of the greatest mental prodigies of all time. But it is far more likely that he did keep *some* notes and that he sent for them from Venice while working on the first draft of the book with Rustichello. Gaps in Marco's memory, plus other factors caused by human error, would account for most of the bewildering compass-bearings given in the *Travels* – Marco was not the only author who ever said east when he meant west! But he was certainly not a skilled navigator himself. Nobody with a basic grasp on celestial navigation could ever have made the error of mentioning a place which is so far north that the Pole Star is south. (This occurs in his discussion of Karakorum and the regions of Mongolia, in the last stage of the outward journey.)

The nickname with which Marco ended his days – *il Milione* – is not altogether unfair, because he certainly did exaggerate. This permeates the *Travels*, and the reader is quite familiar with the fact before Marco has even got further east than Armenia. There are literally scores (if not exactly millions, as Marco would have said) of references to the 'finest city in the world', and other 'finest this, that and the other in the world'. Conversely, it is only fair that Marco's experiences would have made the most polished and articulate writer imaginable run out of accurate superlatives in a very short time. I have suggested that he might have been slightly gullible – decidedly susceptible to the boasts of bazaar-cries and tall stories from other merchants. Yet he was certainly a man of his age in that he was willing to give credence to stories of giant birds killing elephants like seagulls dropping shellfish on to rocks. But

PREVIOUS PAGES Marco Polo: a statuette of him holding a pomegranate, the symbol of wealth and prosperity.

OPPOSITE The site of Marco Polo's house in Venice, now named Corte del Milione after him.

RIGHT The mythical gryphons reported by Marco Polo. His account is a bewildering blend of fact and very definite fiction. From *Le Livre des Merveilles*. BELOW The 'grotesque marvels of India'. From *Les Livres du Graunt Caam* (f 260).

'Messer Marco Polo'

RIGHT An engraving of the 'Noble Knight Marco Polo of Venice, the Great Traveller', from the first German edition of his *Travels* printed in Nuremberg in 1477. This illustration was reproduced in Yule's *The Book of Ser Marco Polo*.

BELOW A portrait of Marco Polo copied from a painting by an unknown artist in the gallery of Monsignore Badia at Rome. This is generally assumed to be the most authentic likeness, although it was executed after Marco's death.

OPPOSITE Marco Polo: a mosaic portrait of 'Il Milione' by Francesco Salviati (1510-53).

there is no reason to disbelieve the claims made by Marco in the Prologue that he deliberately set out to further his status in Kubilai's eyes by telling the Great Khan the sort of things he really wanted to hear. This proves at least that Marco had the mother wit to earn himself success when he saw the chance, and incidentally helps explain why so many miracles and prodigies find their way into the *Travels*. Most of them would have stuck in Marco's mind because they had once formed part of his reports to Kubilai, and because the ensuing discussion or argument cemented many memories.

As far as 'Marco the man' is concerned, many facets of his character are not difficult to define. He had definite charm with an underlying aura of capability. Niccolò and Maffeo were sufficiently impressed by this to take the boy along with them when they set out from Venice on their second journey to Cathay. And certainly Kubilai himself was deeply impressed with Marco – a glowing testimonial to ability from one of the greatest rulers the world has ever seen. Apart from this, Marco was tough. He survived sea voyages, bandit ambushes, disease and above all the fatigue of being more or less constantly on the road for twenty-odd years. He had a puppy-like curiosity about practically everything, including a definite eye for the girls – even the intimate details of Kubilai Khan's personal harem. All in all one envies Rustichello, who must have been infected with Marco's enthusiasm (let alone with his incredible story) while trying to get it all down on paper and improve on the layout of Marco's memories at the same time.

This brings us back to the *Travels* again, and what happened to the book after Marco's death. The basic trouble was that it was a medieval best-seller, and the long-term fate of medieval best-sellers was inevitable distortion, editing and indifferent-to-misleading translations. Modern readers, fortunately, have the benefit of twentieth-century scholarship to help them, most notably that of Professor A. C. Moule and Ronald Latham. The quotations from the *Travels* used in this book are based on the Latham translation. But in the two centuries after the first appearance of the *Travels*, nothing restricted its popularity other than plain old human scepticism. The importance of Marco's book in the history of the world may be gauged by the fact that it inspired Christopher Columbus to set off across the Atlantic to take what he believed to be the direct, short route to Cathay. It was not Marco's fault that the size of the world had been grossly underestimated, and that the West Indies and America got in Columbus's way in consequence.

OPPOSITE The Hereford map of the world, probably compiled by Richard of Haldingham at the end of the thirteenth century. Showing the east at the top, with Jerusalem at the centre, this map follows the typical medieval *mappa-mundi* pattern and does not take into account any of the discoveries of travellers such as Marco Polo.

Part of an Italian map of
1459 based on Marco Polo's
description of Khanbalig.
Outside Khanbalig and
north-west of it lies the
'Heavenly City' of Kinsai.
Marco Polo's *Travels*
revolutionized the medieval
concept of regions hitherto
unexplored, and his
calculations of distances in
terms of days' journeys are
now considered to be fairly
accurate and scientific.

Nor can Marco be blamed for failing to take in the full import of what he saw during his stay in China. He was not intellectually equipped – probably no European of his time was, for that matter – to realize that Kubilai's greatest achievement was the preservation of the entire fabric of Chinese culture, like a fly in amber, in the overall bulk of the Mongol Empire. Thanks to Kubilai's efforts, the genius of China survived the erosion and disappearance of the power he himself had wielded.

What Marco did understand, and what he recorded as fully as any man in his position could ever hope to have done, was the spectacle of the Mongol Empire at its peak. The Polos could never have got to Cathay had it not been for the 'Eurasian *pax*' created and maintained by the Tartar khans. Marco fully recognized this achievement, and his praise swelled at times into enthusiastic hero-worship. But he was enough of a realist to accept the evidence of the march of events. Even before the Polos had got back to Venice, ominous fissures had cracked the Tartar world, and those fissures were never to be repaired.

The Polos heard the news of Kubilai's death while they were still in Persia, in 1294, although throughout the *Travels* he is referred to as if still alive. With the sadness they must have felt at the passing of their generous patron, the Polos must also have experienced relief that the tenacious old man could no longer draw them back into the clutch of his orbit. Kubilai's grandson, Temur, became Great Khan – the sixth Tartar ruler to hold that eminence. He was the second and last effective ruler of the Yüan dynasty founded by Kubilai in the Far East and his rule was short: he died in 1307. The ensuing fifty years saw an unceasing resurgence of Chinese nationalism, culminating with the great revolt of 1368-71 under the leadership of Chu Yüan-chang, first of the Ming emperors, who drove the Mongols out of China. In the West, too, the Mongol supremacy had only fettered Islam, not destroyed it. The ilkhanate of Persia broke up only a few years before the Mongol occupation of China. Nushirwan was the last effective ruler of Mongol Persia and his reign, like that of Temur in Cathay, was a short one, 1344-9.

Thus Marco's account of what he saw is invaluable because of its timing. He saw both the zenith of Tartar power and the start of its inexorable decline.

A final comment on Marco's achievement is to be found in an Epilogue to the *Travels* written by one of his contemporaries in the early fourteenth century as a neater ending to Marco's own somewhat abrupt conclusion. It makes a very good point in

222

stressing the 'happy chance' that enabled the Polos to get out of Cathay when they did, and it ends:

But I believe it was God's will that we should come back, so that men might know the things that are in the world, since, as we have said in the first chapter of this book, no other man, Christian or Saracen, Tartar or pagan, has explored so much of the world as Messer Marco, son of Messer Niccolò Polo, great and noble citizen of the city of Venice.

An eight-faceted porcelain vase of the Yüan dynasty: fourteenth century.

Further Reading

The first essential for the general reader wanting to know more about Marco's achievement is a well edited translation of his *Description of the World*, and by far the best example I have found is available in Penguin Classics. This is published under the title *The Travels of Marco Polo* and is translated and annotated by R. E. Latham.

For background reading on Marco's world there is the lavishly illustrated two-volume edition of *The Shorter Cambridge Medieval History* by Professor C. W. Previté-Orton (Cambridge University Press), which gives a succinct overview of the changing patterns in Europe and the Middle East. The phenomenon of the Tartar conquest of Eurasia and Kubilai Khan's achievement is put equally in perspective in *The Outline of History* – that still-unrivalled history of the world by H. G. Wells. He later overhauled the *Outline* and produced *A Short History of the World*, a considerably handier volume published by Collins Classics.

The two classic commentaries on Marco are: *The Book of Ser Merco Polo the Venetian concerning Kingdoms and Marvels of the East* by Sir Henry Yule (1903) and *Marco Polo: the Description of the World* by A. C. Moule and P. Elliot (1938).

List of Illustrations

2 The Polos leaving Venice,   *Bodleian Library, Oxford*

3 Chinese pottery figure of an actor,   photograph ROBERT HARDING ASSOCIATES, *Peoples' Republic of China*

10–11 Mongol troops crossing a frozen river,   *Radio Times Hulton Picture Library*

12 Jenghiz Khan enthroned,   *Bibliothèque Nationale, Paris*

14 The death of Jenghiz Khan,   *Bibliothèque Nationale, Paris*

14–15 Jenghiz Khan's cavalry,   *Metropolitan Museum of Art, New York.*

15 Mongol warrior plaiting his horse's tail,   *Topkapi Palace Museum, Istanbul*

17 Jenghiz Khan seated in a mosque at Bukhara,   *Bibliothèque Nationale, Paris*

18 Jenghiz Khan with his sons,   *Bibliothèque Nationale, Paris*

20 Arabs and Christians in battle,   *MAS, Barcelona*

21 Crusader knight doing homage,   *British Museum*

22–3 Aerial view of Krak des Chevaliers,   *Aerofilms*

24–5 Crusaders departing for the Holy Land,   *British Museum*

25 Knight receiving his sword from the king,   *Durham Cathedral Library*

28–9 Hulagu feasts before leaving Mongolia to invade Persia,   *The Warburg Institute*

32–3 The Eastern Orthodox Chapel of Calvary in the Church of the Holy Sepulchre at Jerusalem,   *Middle East Archive*

34 Detail from a twelfth-century map of Crusader Jerusalem,   *Bibliothèque Cambrai* and *Giraudon*

36 Portrait of Kubilai Khan,   photograph JOHN FREEMAN, *British Museum*

39 Tartar warrior,   *Radio Times Hulton Picture Library*

40 The Doge and clergy praying,   photograph JOSEPHINE POWELL

42 Pope Gregory x,   *Mansell Collection*

43 The Piazzetta at Venice,   photograph JOHN FREEMAN, *British Museum*

44–5 The Polos setting off from Venice, 1271,   *Bibliothèque Nationale, Paris*

46–7 The Christians alarmed at the Caliph's words,   *Bodleian Library, Oxford*

48 The citadel of Aleppo,   *Werner Forman Archive*

50–1 Travellers in Armenia,   *Bibliothèque Nationale, Paris*

57 The 'Golden Friday Mosque', Baghdad,   *Werner Forman Archive*

59 Marco hears the story of the three kings,   *Bodleian Library, Oxford*

60 Wild ass of Mongolia,   photograph JOHN FREEMAN, *British Museum*

62 Nomad travellers,   *Topkapi Palace Museum, Istanbul*

63 Mongol warriors besieging a city,   *Bibliothèque Nationale, Paris*

64 Giraffe and figures at Tabriz,   *Radio Times Hulton Picture Library*

66–7 Camel caravans transporting wood,   *Camera Press Ltd*

70–1 Brigands attack travellers,   *Bibliothèque Nationale, Paris*

74 Masyaf Castle,   *Werner Forman Archive*

75 'A garden like Paradise',   *Bodleian Library, Oxford*

76–7 Assassins killing Nizam al-Mulk,   *Topkapi Palace Museum, Istanbul*

78–9 The siege of Baghdad by Hulagu,   *Mansell Collection*

81 The great river Balacian,   *Bodleian Library, Oxford*

82–3 Autumn on the Pamirs in Sinkiang,   *Camera Press Ltd*

225

84 *Ovis Poli,* photograph JOHN FREEMAN, *British Museum*
86–7 The Gobi Desert, *Camera Press Ltd*
88–9 Camels in Mongolia, *Camera Press Ltd*
92 (*Top*) Camel caravan in north China, *Werner Forman Archive*
92 (*Bottom*) A modern Mongol with his pony, *Camera Press Ltd*
93 (*Top*) Mongols on horseback, *Camera Press Ltd*
93 (*Bottom*) Mongolian horsemen ready for hurdle-race, *Collection Viollet*
96 The Great Wall of China, *Camera Press Ltd*
99 The battle of Jenghiz Khan and Prester John, *Bodleian Library, Oxford*
101 One of Jenghiz Khan's battles, *Mansell Collection*
102 The capture of a Chinese town by Jenghiz Khan, *Mansell Collection*
104–5 The Altai Mountains in western Mongolia, *Camera Press Ltd*
106–7 Mongolian yurts, *Camera Press Ltd*
108 The god of the Tartars, *Bodleian Library, Oxford*
109 A Mongol bowman on horseback, *Photo Harlingue-Viollet*
111 Papal letters being presented to the Khan, *Bodleian Library, Oxford*
112–13 Peking, *Collection Viollet*
114 Watchtower on the walls of Peking, *Werner Forman Archive*
117 (*Top*) A sun-dial in Peking, *Camera Press Ltd*
117 (*Bottom*) The walls of the palace in Peking, *Camera Press Ltd*
122–3 Aerial view of the mountains of Afghanistan, *Werner Forman Archive*
123 The entrance to the palace district of the Khans in Ulan Bator, *Werner Forman Archive*
125 Hawking, *Radio Times Hulton Picture Library*
126–7 Mongolian horsemen lassoing animals, *Camera Press Ltd*
127 An archer of Kubilai's period, *Mansell Collection*
128 Medieval Tartar huts and wagons, photograph JOHN FREEMAN, *British Museum*
129 A Mongolian bell-tower, with yurts in the foreground, *Camera Press Ltd*
131 The Khan distributes alms, *Bodleian Library, Oxford*
132 The Khan hunts deer, *Bodleian Library, Oxford*
134–5 The Khan and three of his wives, *Bodleian Library, Oxford*
135 The Khan's birthday party, *Bodleian Library, Oxford*
136–7 The Khan crossing a bridge of boats, *Warburg Institute*
140–1 The courtyard of the temple of Kuan-siao, *Werner Forman Archive*
144–5 The Chü-yang Gate, *Werner Forman Archive*
147 The bridge of Pulisanghin, photograph JOHN FREEMAN, *British Museum*
148–9 Hsi-ling Gorge on Yangtse-kiang, *Camera Press Ltd*
150 The garden-house on the lake at Yunnan-fu, photograph JOHN FREEMAN, *British Museum*
153 Elephants with castles of wood for war, *Bibliothèque Nationale, Paris*
154–5 Three details from the 'Spring on the River' scroll, *Palace Museum, Peking* and *Werner Forman Archive*
156 The residential city of the Burmese kings at Pagan, *Werner Forman Archive*
159 The gold and silver towers of Pagan, *Bodleian Library, Oxford*

226

162 Silver harness ornament, photograph ROBERT HARDING ASSOCIATES, *Peoples' Republic of China*

163 The city of Kinsai, *Bodleian Library, Oxford*

165 The Khan presents his golden tablets, *Bodleian Library, Oxford*

166 Stoneware pillow, photograph ROBERT HARDING ASSOCIATES, *Peoples' Republic of China*

167 (*Left*) White glazed porcelain bottle, photograph ROBERT HARDING ASSOCIATES, *Peoples' Republic of China*

167 (*Right*) Porcelain ewer and bowl, photograph ROBERT HARDING ASSOCIATES, *Peoples' Republic of China*

168 Arghun, ruler of Persia, *Bibliothèque Nationale, Paris*

170–1 A typhoon off the Along coast, *Werner Forman Archive*

172 Ch'u-fu temple district in Shantung province, *Werner Forman Archive*

175 A Buddhist cemetery in Shantung, *Werner Forman Archive*

176 Indian ships at Zaiton, *Bodleian Library, Oxford*

177 The Wat Po temple, Bangkok, *Collection Viollet*

178 Medieval ships in the Java seas, photograph JOHN FREEMAN, *British Museum*

182 Stone figure at Madras, *Werner Forman Archive*

184–5 Indian landscape at Trivandrum, *Werner Forman Archive*

188–9 The title page to Henry Yule's *The Book of Ser Marco Polo*, *Radio Times Hulton Picture Library*

190 Miniature of a Persian princess, *Radio Times Hulton Picture Library*

192–3 Marco Polo disembarks at Hormuz, *Collection Viollet*

196 A gryphon dropping elephants, photograph JOHN FREEMAN, *British Museum*

199 An Ethiopian sheep, photograph JOHN FREEMAN, *British Museum*

200 Persian silver inlaid bowls, *Radio Times Hulton Picture Library*

201 Persian bronze basin, *Radio Times Hulton Picture Library*

202–3 Sailing ships in the Andamans, *Bibliothèque Nationale, Paris*

203 Pearl fishing in the gulf of Malabar, *Bodleian Library, Oxford*

206–7 Marco Polo at the battle of Curzola, photograph JOHN FREEMAN, *British Museum*

207 Marco Polo telling his story to Rustichello, *Radio Times Hulton Picture Library*

208 Campo San Lorenzo, *Civici Musei Veneziani d'Arte e di Storia*

209 The last Will of Marco Polo, photograph JOHN FREEMAN, *British Museum*

210–11 Model of Marco Polo, *Museo Correr, Venice* and *Werner Forman Archive*

212 Corte del Milione, *Werner Forman Archive*

214–15 Gryphons, *Bibliothèque Nationale, Paris*

214 The 'grotesque marvels of India', *Bodleian Library, Oxford*

216 (*Top*) Marco Polo, engraving, photograph JOHN FREEMAN, *British Museum*

227

216 (*Bottom*) Marco Polo, engraving from painting, *Radio Times Hulton Picture Library*

217 Marco Polo, mosaic by Francesco Salviati, *Palazzo Comunale, Genoa* and *Mansell Collection*

218 The Hereford map of the world, *Mansell Collection*

220–1 A map based on Marco Polo's description of Khanbalig, *British Museum*

223 Porcelain vase, photograph ROBERT HARDING ASSOCIATES, *Peoples' Republic of China*

Picture research by Pat Hodgson.

The maps on pages 52, 118–19 and 179 were drawn by Design Practitioners Ltd.

Index

Abaka Khan, 204–5
Abyssinia, 197–8
Acre, 26, 30, 39, 41, 45, 53
Aden, 197–8
Ahmad, 143, 146, 160
Ain Jalut, battle of (1260), 16, 49
Aiyaruk, Princess, 204
Alexander IV, Pope, 13, 19, 36–8,
    41
Amou, 169
Arabia, 198
Aral Sea, 16, 26, 84
Arghun, Ilkhan of Persia, 186,
    198–9, 204–5
Armenia, 49, 54, 65, 80, 205, 213
Assassins, 73, 75, 78–9
Ayas, 39, 41–2, 49, 54, 65, 73

Badakhshan, 79–81, 85
Baghdad, 16, 39, 55–6, 58, 73,
    78–9, 196
Baldwin, Emperor of
    Constantinople, 27
Balkash, Lake, 26
Balkh, 79
Barak, 30
Barka Khan, 27, 30, 44, 54
Basra, 58, 65
Batu Khan, 13, 16
Bengal, Bay of, 173, 180
Bibars, Sultan of Egypt, 49
Bintang, 174
Black Sea, 27, 205–6
Bolgana, Queen of Persia, 186
Borneo, 174
Buddhism, 133, 138, 173, 180
Bukhara, 30–1, 35, 39, 79, 85
Bundukdari, Sultan of Egypt, 49, 54
Burma, 146, 152, 157–8

Caspian Sea, 26, 30, 54, 79, 200
Cathay, see China
Caucasus, 16, 54
Ceylon, 173, 180–1, 183, 191, 198

Chagatai Khan, 89–90
Charchan, 90–1
Ch'ien-hu, 143
China, 13, 16, 31, 35, 37, 42, 45, 53,
    58, 64–5, 79–80, 90, 95, 97, 103,
    109–10, 115, 120, 131–2, 138,
    139, 143, 146, 150, 158, 160–1,
    162–3, 169, 173–4, 182, 186, 198,
    200, 219, 222
Chinkim, Prince, 120–1, 143
Christianity, 19, 36–8, 44, 53, 56,
    89–90, 97–8, 100, 103, 115, 162,
    173, 180, 195, 197–8
Constantinople, 24, 26–7, 205
Crimea, 16, 26–7
Crusades, 19, 24

Damascus, 49, 79
Danube, River, 16, 26

Egypt, 16, 24, 49, 198
Erzincan, 54, 65
Essen Temur, 151
Euphrates, River, 49
Europe, 13, 16, 19, 35–7, 115, 130,
    133, 138, 157

France, 26, 187
Fu-chow, 162, 169

Georgia, 54–5, 58, 61
Ghazan, Prince of Persia, 199–201,
    205
Gobi Desert, 26, 35, 85, 90–1, 94–5,
    167
Golden Horde, 16, 26–7, 44
Great Wall of China, 35, 97–8, 146
Gregory x, Pope, 41–5, 49, 53, 97

Hangchow, 162–4, 167
Holy Land, 19, 41, 43, 79

Hormuz, 58–9, 64–5, 68–9, 72, 80, 91, 173–4, 191, 194–5, 198–9
Hukaji Khan, 151
Hulagu Khan, 16, 30, 38, 49, 54–6, 58, 79
Hwang-ho, River, 147, 160–1

India, 58, 60, 65, 68, 72–3, 151, 162, 169, 173, 181, 186, 191, 198
Indian Ocean, 72, 195, 197
Innocent IV, Pope, 26
Irrawaddy, River, 152, 158–9
Isfahan, 200
Ishkasham, 79

Japan, 174
Java, 174
Jenghiz Khan, 13, 16, 26, 35, 98–100, 103, 109
Jerusalem, 26, 38, 41, 197

Kaidu Khan, 89–90, 201, 204
Kaikhatu Khan, 198–200
Kamadin, 68
Kamul, 95
Kanchow, 97
Kara-jang, 142, 146, 151–2
Karakorum, 13, 26, 37, 97, 201, 213
Karaunas, 68–9, 73
Kashgar, 35, 85, 88, 90
Kashmir, 80, 115
Kerman, 61, 64, 68, 72–3, 80
Khanbalig, 35, 38, 44, 120, 124, 127, 143, 146, 158, 160, 180, 186–7, 198
Khotan, 90–1
Kogatai, 143, 146
Kogatai, Baron, 38–9
Kokachin, Princess, 186, 191, 199–200, 205
Kubilai Khan, 15, 19, 25–7, 30–1, 35–9, 41, 43–4, 56, 68, 85, 89, 94–5, 103, 110, 115, 120–1, 124,

126–8, 130–1, 133, 138–9, 142–3, 146–7, 151–2, 158, 160–2, 164, 169, 173–4, 180–1, 183, 186–7, 196, 198, 200–1, 204, 219, 222
Kuyuk Khan, 13

Liegnitz, battle of (1241), 13, 16
Li-tan, 161
Lop, 90–1
Louis IX, King of France, 26

Maarbar, 181–3, 197
Madagascar, 195–6
Malabar, 191, 194
Malay, 174
Mamluks, 16, 49, 54–5, 58, 65, 198
Mangalai Khan, 147
Mangu Khan, 13, 16, 26, 95, 103, 150
Manzi, 160–2, 169, 173–4, 191
Mediterranean, 21, 39, 49, 65, 131, 205
Mesopotamia, 16, 49, 54–6, 58, 65
Mongol Empire, 13, 16, 26, 35, 43, 73, 91, 124, 198, 222
Mongolia, 13, 26, 97–8, 201, 213
Moslems, 24, 56, 61, 75, 89–90, 146, 197, 204
Mosul, 56, 58
Mulehet, 73, 79

Nicholas of Vicenza, Brother, 43, 49, 53–4, 73
Nigudar, 68
Numughan, Prince, 201

Ogadai Khan, 13, 16
Orda Khan, 26
Oxus, River, 84

230

Pagan, 152, 158
Pamir, 84–5, 167
Pashai, 80
Pem, 90–1
Persia, 13, 16, 49, 54, 58, 60, 65, 73, 78, 180, 186, 199, 201, 205, 222
Persian Gulf, 58, 68, 191, 198
Piano Carpini, Giovanni di, 26–7, 31, 97
Polo, Maffeo, 25–7, 30–1, 35–9, 41–2, 44–5, 49, 54–5, 58–61, 64–5, 68–9, 72–3, 79–80, 84–5, 88–91, 94, 97, 110–11, 115, 130–2, 161–2, 173–4, 182, 186–7, 191, 194–5, 198–200, 205, 219, 222–3
Polo, Marco, account of Polos' first journey, 27, 30–1, 35–8; leaves Venice, 41; and Pope Gregory, 42–3; leaves Acre, 45; stopped by Mamluks, 49, 54; describes journey to Hormuz, 54–6, 58–61, 64, 68–9, 72–3; returns to Persia, 73; his illness and recovery, 79–80; describes journey to China, 80–1, 84–5, 88–91, 94–5; story of Prester John, 98–100, 103; account of Tartar life, 103, 106–10; meets Kubilai Khan, 110–11; describes Shang-tu and Khanbalig, 115–16, 120–1, 124–8, 130–3, 138–9, 142–4; and attempted *coup*, 143, 146; journey to Kara-jang, 146–9, 150–2; returns, 158–60; journey to Manzi, 160–4, 166–7, 169; voyage to Ceylon, 173–4, 176, 178, 190; in India, 181–3, 186; leaves China, 187; sails to Hormuz, 191; in Persia, 200–1; describes Tartar Wars, 201, 204–5; returns to Venice, 205; death, 206, 209; and the *Travels*, 213, 219; describes legends of countries on his journeys, 55–6,

89–90, 97, 157–8; character, 65, 115, 206, 219; achievement, 222–3
Polo, Niccolò, 25–7, 30–1, 35–9, 41–2, 44–5, 49, 54–5, 58–61, 64–5, 68–9, 72–3, 79–80, 84–5, 88–91, 94, 97, 110–11, 115, 130–2, 142, 161–2, 173–4, 182, 186–7, 191, 194–5, 198–200, 205, 219, 222–3
Ponte, Messer, 27
Prester John, 97–8, 100, 103, 146, 201, 204

Rome, 37, 41
Roubrouck, Guillaume de, 26–7, 31, 97–8, 108
Rudbar, 68–9, 73
Rustichello, Messer, 94, 97–8, 157, 204–5, 213

Samarkand, 35, 79, 89–90, 201
Saveh, 58–9, 65
Shang-tu, 16, 110, 115–16, 143
Shibarghan, 79
Singapore, 174
Sirikol, Lake, 84
Suchow, 94–5, 97
Sudak, 26–7, 30
Sumatra, 173–4, 176, 180, 191
Syria, 16, 49
Szechwan, 16, 150–1

Tabriz, 58, 64–5, 200
Talikhan, 79
Tangut, 94–5, 110
Tartars, 13, 16, 19, 24–7, 30, 37, 49, 54–6, 60–1, 68, 73, 79, 84, 95, 97–9, 103, 106–110, 116, 124–5, 130, 142, 146, 152, 157–8, 163, 174, 187, 201, 222
Temur Khan, 120, 222
Tibet, 115, 150–1

231

Tiflis, 55, 65
Tigris, River, 58, 65
Togrul Khan, 98
Travels, 35, 54, 56, 64, 69, 80,
    94–5, 97–8, 103, 111, 115, 124,
    142–3, 146, 151, 157–8, 160–1,
    167, 173, 182, 186, 194, 201,
    205–6, 213, 219, 222
Turkestan, 26, 73, 90, 98, 198, 201

Venice, 19, 21, 24–5, 27, 37, 41, 65,
    89, 205, 213, 219, 222–3
Volga, River, 16, 26–7, 30

Wan-hu, 143
White Horde, 26
William, Brother, of Tripoli, 43, 49,
    53–4, 73

Yangchow, 161–2
Yangtse-Kiang, River, 146–7, 151,
    160, 162
Yazd, 59, 61, 65

Zaiton, 173–4, 186–7
Zanzibar, 195, 197